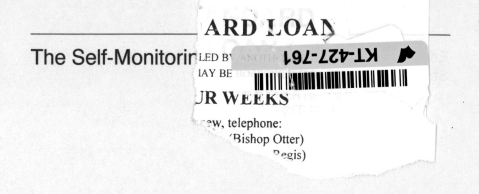

The Self-Monitorin

Educational management series
Series editor: Cyril Poster

The Self-Monitoring Primary School

Edited by Pearl White and Cyril Poster

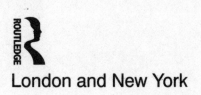

London and New York

First published 1997
by Routledge
11 New Fetter Lane, London EC4P 4EE

Simultaneously published in the USA and Canada
by Routledge
29 West 35th Street, New York, NY 10001

Typeset in Palatino by
Keystroke, Jacaranda Lodge, Wolverhampton

Printed and bound in Great Britain by
Clays Ltd, St Ives plc

British Library Cataloguing in Publication Data
A catalogue record for this book is available from the British Library

Library of Congress Cataloguing in Publication Data
A catalogue record for this book has been requested

ISBN 0–415–14817–0

Contents

Figures

Introduction

Cyril Poster

Cyril Poster was for thirty-five years a secondary school teacher, and for twenty-five of them successively founding headteacher of two comprehensive schools and principal of a Leicestershire community college. He retired from teaching to become deputy director of the National Development Centre for School Management Training at Bristol University and then a freelance trainer and consultant. For the past ten years he has been series editor of the Routledge Educational Management series.

When we look back at the 1990s we will undoubtedly judge it to be the decade in which more radical change took place than at any time in the history of British education. The rate of change has been bewildering to those who have had to implement it, and even more so to parents and the general public, despite a plethora of charters and publicity.

School governors suddenly found themselves with responsibilities, for which they were legally liable, that were entirely new to them and for which they were ill-prepared and, if trained at all, inadequately so. The National Curriculum as a concept has much to commend it in a society of high and increasing mobility; but its advantages were offset by three years of repeated revisions to curriculum content which left many headteachers wondering, as a new batch of documents arrived on their desks, why they had spent so much time and energy planning the implementation of the last, superseded batch. The introduction of published league tables for public examinations, closely followed by those for the levels of attainment in Key Stages 1–3, told schools in the leafy suburbs what they already knew, and signalled to inner city schools that their efforts to prepare their pupils for life were insignificant compared with how close they could get to the national averages in tests, the sole purpose of which is the measurement of achievement.

The introduction of local financial management proved to be a measure that, once headteachers and school secretaries had learnt budgetary skills, was initially of benefit to schools. More recently, as reductions in the money available began to lead to cuts in staffing and materials, and ever increasing problems of building maintenance, there may well be regrets that LEAs can no longer help out from retained funds. Furthermore, many schools now find themselves having to pay for LEA training and advisory services, the need for which has increased with each new implementation of government policy.

The concept of LEA advice and support has been replaced by that of external inspection. Her Majesty's Inspectorate, after a worthy history extending over a century and a half, was replaced by the Office for Standards in Education (OFSTED). Many schools that valued the expertise of HMI inspections despite their searching nature, now began to dread inspections that were to brand some schools as 'failing' and large numbers of teachers as inefficient.

Against this background of school education in shades of black and grey, it is remarkable that so many schools have not merely survived but have themselves initiated processes and devised roles to give them ownership of their own development. Self-monitoring is one means to this end. It differs from inspection, as the contributor to chapter 2 points out, principally in that it is not judgmental, and from appraisal in that it looks at wider issues than staff effectiveness and staff development.

The self-monitoring school is a logical extension of the effective school movement that derived from the International School Improvement Project (ISIP) of the mid-1980s and of the self-managing school, increasingly to be found in Australia, New Zealand and some states of the USA (Caldwell and Spinks 1988).

Self-monitoring is, above all, a means by which a school can develop strategies for improvement and, in particular, the means to implement them. It is able to control the pace of such development by effective communication and shared decision-making within the staff, and to win support for what it is doing by carrying governors and parents with it, stage by stage.

Monitoring, and self-monitoring above all, needs to be distinguished from evaluation, though the professional literature often treats monitoring and evaluation as portmanteau words, as did the School Management Task Force (DES 1990). Evaluation, according to Aspinwall *et al.* (1992:13), is most commonly viewed as part of the planning cycle. They cite Hargreaves *et al.* (1989:5) who identified four Key Stages in the cycle:

- *Audit*: where a school reviews its strengths and weaknesses
- *Plan construction*: where priorities for development are selected and become specific targets
- *Implementation* of the planned priorities and targets; and
- *Evaluation*: where the success of implementation is checked

This definition is, as the contributors to this book demonstrate, insufficiently proactive for the self-monitoring school, which requires a regular routine review of what is actually happening in classroom and school management. The first five chapters, each from a different perspective, are at one in demonstrating the ongoing interaction between the self-monitoring process and improved performance, particularly in the establishment of policies, planning and procedures (chapter 3), and the actual processes by which monitoring is conducted, in the school (chapter 4) and the classroom (chapter 5).

Not least of the merits of self-monitoring is that it empowers schools by enabling them to establish the rate at which processes and procedures are introduced, and to prioritise the stages by which outcomes will be realised. It may be that some readers of this book, attracted initially by the concept of self-monitoring, take fright at its apparent complexity. It must be emphasised that chapter 4, for example, represents developments in one school over several years and, most importantly, took all the members of staff along with it at every stage. Self-monitoring *can* be imposed by senior management, but it is unlikely to be effective if the decision to introduce it is not taken collegially.

The fact that this book is about the experience of self-monitoring in the primary school should not deter those in secondary schools from reading it and considering its application to their phase. There is nothing here that is not equally applicable or adaptable to larger schools with different management structures. It is simply that the five contributors working in primary schools felt it important that they spoke directly of their own experience, a decision which the editors and the two advisers, writing specifically about special educational needs in the self-monitoring school (chapter 6) and the supporting role of the LEA (chapter 7) recognised as entirely appropriate.

It may be that this book will make an even more important contribution to the management of schools than when it was first conceived. There is every likelihood that external inspection will be modified either by political decision or because of cost. The task of four-yearly inspection of over 30,000 schools cannot be maintained by the existing number of qualified inspectors. If it comes about that inspection is reserved for schools deemed to be failing, and for an annual sample of other schools, then self-monitoring will be of even greater importance. Already the *Framework for Inspection 1996* is requiring schools subject to inspection to give not only background details, but also to cite what measures they have in place for internal 'evaluation'. Much of the threat seen by many schools in the inspectorial approach will be minimised if they are able, having established self-monitoring procedures, to put forward their own view of their successes and shortcomings.

Chapter 1

The purpose of monitoring

Pearl White

Pearl White's teaching career has been wholly in the West Midlands. Her qualifications include a B.Phil. (Ed.) and her original specialism was in early years education, with a particular concern for special educational needs. During a career break to raise three daughters she served as a part-time college lecturer training NNEB students. After her return to full-time teaching she was soon appointed headteacher of her present school, Kates Hill Primary School. In recognition of her contribution to curriculum innovation she was in 1993 awarded an Associate Fellowship by the University of Wolverhampton. She is a Registered Inspector for OFSTED and spent 1995–6 on secondment as an additional inspector.

What makes a 'good school' good now, as the twentieth century draws to a close? Is it one that values every individual, adult or pupil, associated with the school? Or is it one that aims to develop good self-esteem in staff and pupils, one that believes that it is offering 'education for life' for the whole community of staff, pupils and parents?

All teachers within a good school would agree that at the centre are the pupils whose individual needs are of paramount importance. The pupils need to be enjoying their learning and their achievement must obviously be valued. Teachers should have understanding about how pupils learn and be able to provide a range of teaching strategies, be well organised and have high expectations of their pupils. It is essential that there is strong, reliable educational leadership by the headteacher, one which combines clear vision with a discerning overview and insight into all the happenings in the school. There need to be clear lines of communication and effective administration. The governors should be enablers, offering unstinting support to all teachers, pupils and parents. Good relationships are vital.

In the latter part of this decade 'raising standards' has become the dominant theme of politicians and educationalists alike. They see good schools as those that are achieving this by introducing baseline testing for five-year-old pupils, and education development plans for schools, with agreed targets for improving standards and attendance. Schools are also being encouraged to become good by developing their assessment techniques and monitoring their value-added analysis of their test and examination results. It is to be hoped that 'good' schools will be seen in the future as those which are improving year by year on their present best.

What makes a good school has been taxing the minds of educationalists over many decades. Politicians, parents, the wider society and, not least, all those involved as educators have a desire to improve and develop the quality of teaching and learning so that all aspects of pupil achievement and development are enhanced. There has been a great change in the level of expectation in recent years. Parents want their children to obtain better qualifications and, as the number of available jobs declines and the nature of work changes radically, employers put pressure on schools to provide a better qualified workforce.

Since the early 1980s there has been a rapid growth in research which tries to identify 'what makes a good school good now'. The investigation has fallen into two main areas: school effectiveness and school improvement. Researchers such as Rutter *et al.* (1979) have examined the quality of schooling in order to find out why some schools are more effective than others in fostering positive outcomes. Regrettably, positive outcomes are seen now to be largely measured by Standard Assessment Test results. We now have league tables of test and examination results in both primary and secondary schools and it is argued that these, together with the Office for Standards In Education (OFSTED) inspections, are able to identify good schools. Is it surprising that schools at the top of the league tables are ones whose pupils come from socially advantaged homes: parents in professional occupations and minimal unemployment in the area? As many educationalists know, examination results cannot evaluate whole school success, as they do not take into account the value-added element that many schools provide. Pupils enter schools at five at varying stages of development, emotionally, socially, physically and intellectually, and progress at an individual rate. As yet there is no known measure to gauge the progress made by pupils towards these outcomes. A successful school is one that aids all pupils to develop to their full potential. Effective schools are ones that take action to improve their pupils' performance by setting targets against which their progress is monitored. Target setting, of course, cannot alone improve schools. As Barth (1990) argues, the school 'culture' has to be improved so that the conditions are right for learning to be promoted and sustained. To achieve this is the responsibility of school managers.

Other researchers (for example, Louis and Miles 1990 and Hopkins *et al.* 1994) have studied the processes that schools go through to become more productive. They seek to find out what schools do to make themselves more successful, to provide a better education for all their pupils.

What steps do schools take to help them to provide a better service to their pupils, parents and wider society?

There continues to exist a divide between the two schools of thought on effectiveness and improvement. The belief of Reynolds and Creemers (1990: 2) is that, although there is much understanding about what makes a school good, our ability to use the knowledge does not match this under-standing. Research into school improvement, however, does give us a valuable insight into how to make schools more effective. Practitioners are empirical: they take the results of research from both traditions to aid them in their efforts to make their schools good.

This interest in school effectiveness and school improvement is manifested in the attention that is paid to whole-school development, innovation and self-evaluation (Bolam 1982; Hopkins and Wideen 1984; McMahon *et al*. 1984). There is no point in analysing practice unless it is going to lead to remodelling and consequently to changing procedures and promoting actions that influence the school to improve. The impor-tant concept implicit in all the research is that self-evaluation and self-review are of paramount importance. There has to be a motivating force for improvement: therefore all staff need to be involved and to share in the desired outcomes. Rodger and Richardson portray a self-evaluating school as follows:

> It is a school in which staff see themselves as part of a collaborative venture aimed at the purposeful education of children . . . [one] which is prepared to devote precious time and energy to reflective activities . . . Above all it is a school that has a genuine desire to find out about itself and by so doing to make itself a better place for young children to develop.
>
> (Rodger and Richardson 1985: 20–1)

Whole-school evaluation will not automatically bring about improvement. For this there must be change in policies, schemes, teaching strategies and management. The self-reviewing school has to be at the centre of change activities.

There is now a significant body of research knowledge that identifies the various mechanisms that underpin effectiveness. This information is consolidated in the publication *Governing Bodies and Effective Schools* (1995) which consolidates the work of many researchers (Rutter *et al*. 1979; Reynolds 1982; Mortimore *et al*. 1988). Extensive research and school inspection evidence show that effective schools share certain features: good leadership with clear vision, a concentration on teaching and learning with high expectations, the creation of a stimulating learning environment and involvement of parents, monitoring whole-school and individual pupil progress, are all key factors in schools that are seen to succeed. This book concerns itself primarily with monitoring progress, a process which underpins the successful achievement of all the school's goals.

The problem remains. How can those in schools find time to add yet another task to the many imposed upon them? There is an awareness of the need to review continually and this process begins by having the knowledge of where we are now. To do this requires policies and systems that enable us routinely to glean information. Review or evaluation is a summative judgment, a snapshot of a school at one point in time. To improve from this point, schools can plan a new direction, can set long-term aims, with specific tasks and targets. To ensure that these tasks and targets are achieved they will have to be regularly checked, that is, monitored.

It is well known that people only engage in change when they are convinced that it is necessary. This truism is at the heart of self-review and evaluation. Similarly, schools, which after all consist of individuals, will only adopt change procedures when they are seen to be essential. Pollard and Tann (1987) refer to 'reflective action', a willingness to engage in constant self-appraisal and development. Reflective teachers have an active concern for improving, desiring to be better teachers. The only way that they can begin to do this is first to learn where they are. This is the first stage in any monitoring process. Stenhouse (1975) argued that teachers should act as researchers of their own practice developing the curriculum through practical enquiry. Similarly, reflective teachers within the reflective school will monitor, observe and collect data on their own and each others' actions. This evidence can then form a data base which can be critically analysed and evaluated. The information gleaned can then be shared by all staff so that judgments can be made on how to improve. It is imperative that the mechanism for monitoring becomes central to the school's organisation and management.

DEFINING MONITORING

Monitoring is continuous, a formative, diagnostic assessment of any activity or performance. It is central to any evaluation process. Having monitored, the school must then take action to ensure that it is on course towards the desired goals. Monitoring is therefore a means of reviewing, regulating and taking appropriate action to aid the satisfactory completion of tasks. A monitor checks, oversees, and keeps a continuous record of any observations made. In a school that is self-monitoring each member of staff has this role.

Monitoring is a term often coupled with other activities: monitoring and control, monitoring and evaluation, monitoring and review. Monitoring is the one common factor in all these activities, fundamental to a constant understanding of what is happening in the education of the pupils. It is central to the cycle of continuous advancement. Monitoring involves keeping a constant check that teachers are doing what they aim to do, that they are on track to deliver the best education possible, that all the policies and procedures are being followed.

Monitoring and control are closely interlinked: a set of operations involved in implementing plans towards desired end results. To control effectively presupposes a willingness to take action and consequently regulate. Objectives, targets, criteria for success, may be in the school development plan, but it is only by constant checking and putting in control mechanisms that there is any guarantee that the desired outcome is being achieved. Sustained observation will lead to success in achieving targets.

A number of terms related to monitoring recur frequently in the literature of school evaluation and improvement: auditing, evaluation and review. There is, however, some inconsistency in the ways these terms are used. For the purpose of this book, which is centred on monitoring in the self-monitoring school, the following distinctions are made:

- *Auditing* is an inspection, a verification, a summative assessment. Any properly documented process can be audited, to check that the system is doing what it is saying it is doing and giving written evidence to prove it.
- *Evaluation* is a general term used to describe any activity where the quality of the provision is the subject of systematic study. When we evaluate we make a judgment about the effectiveness of this activity.
- *Review* is a retrospective activity and implies the collection and examination of evidence and information.

WHY MONITOR?

There is a growing demand, both within the school system and from society at large, for schools to investigate the success or otherwise of their educational policies and practice. Schools are always being encouraged to formulate plans so that they can become constantly improving organisations. Raising standards and improved performance can be aided by whole school review and evaluation, but only if monitoring is embedded in its processes.

Schools' aims are being documented in the much increased paperwork of development plans, parents' brochures and policies. Monitoring of these aims is essential, to ensure that policy is evident in practice and that schemes and guidelines are adhered to. It is imperative that there is confirmation through observation of the teaching and learning that the schemes and guidelines are influencing practice. Checking, by staff, of the implementation of the school development plan is imperative to ensure the achievement of goals and targets.

The gathering of information is one of the responsibilities of a school's central management and, for this, good communication systems are essential. All staff – the headteacher, curriculum coordinators, class teachers, special needs support teachers and administrative staff – need to be involved in the assembling, collation and sharing of data. These procedures will play a significant part in motivating staff by involving them in the decision-making processes. It will also increase the efficiency of managers in their allocation of resources, staff, accommodation, time and finance.

Headteachers gain a detailed knowledge of the working of the school, particularly when visiting classrooms through their monitoring process. As they move about they will seek to ensure that they are providing a secure learning environment for the pupils, one that is bright, exciting and stimulating. To guarantee that all pupils in school have their entitlement to the best educational provision, staff, and particularly headteachers, need to monitor to ensure the delivery of statutory requirements, including the National Curriculum, assessment, recording, procedures for reporting to parents and adhering to the Code of Practice. Schools must be vigilant over the quality of teaching, the opportunities for learning and the curriculum provision. Careful monitoring of pupils' work will show if there is continuity and progression in the pupils' learning.

The personal, professional, developmental and training needs of staff are identified in part through an in-depth examination of the school's success as a teaching and learning institution. Meeting these needs will support appraisal and staff development. It is also through monitoring linked to auditing and review, and thence to further planning, that curriculum areas will be identified for development.

There is an increase in the public accountability of schools, particularly through the publication of league tables of test and examination results and OFSTED reports on schools. Constant checking, through the monitoring process, will give the evidence necessary for schools to be more accountable to the school's clients – pupils, parents, the community and industry – for the quality of education on offer, the standards achieved, the learning taking place and the efficiency of the organisation. Heads are ultimately responsible for standards and the quality of work; but all staff have responsibility for the curriculum they deliver in the classroom and the subjects they coordinate. It follows, therefore, that there has to be whole-staff involvement and commitment to the process of monitoring.

External pressures

Schools have changed greatly since the mid-1980s: in their management, in meeting the demands of the National Curriculum and legislation, and, not least, in the roles and responsibilities of all staff and of governors.

Teachers have the pressure of delivering an ever-changing curriculum to children born into the age of technology and increasingly influenced by the media. Headteachers also have a far more difficult task than in previous decades, with tremendous pressures on them to improve the quality and standards of education in their schools. There is pressure from politicians, parents and the media for schools to be seen to improve what are now widely known as their performance indicators: test and examination results and inspection reports. Schools are taking internal measures of many kinds to provide the public with what they want. This book will provide ideas, techniques and procedures which will aid schools in monitoring, checking and controlling their progress. Nevertheless headteachers face enormous external pressures by way of recommendations and legislation sent from central government, to which they have to respond.

The changing role of the headteacher

Since the Education Reform Act (1988), the many alterations in legislation and the introduction of new and amended regulations have radically changed the role of the headteacher. This was predicted by Coopers and Lybrand (1988) who said the introduction of self-management of schools would have a major impact, with a new culture and philosophy being established in schools. Although the first element of change was the introduction of local financial management (LFM) the totality of change has been more than merely financial. The greatest change is in the roles and responsibilities of headteachers, staff and governors. The policies for local management of schools (LMS) were next introduced to increase the autonomy of schools in relation to their governance and it was this that significantly remodelled the whole role of the head-teacher.

Headteachers were in the past largely paternal managers, fully involved in all aspects of the life of their schools. Before schools, both primary and secondary, grew to their present size, headteachers might well claim to know all the children and their capabilities and, certainly in primary schools, taught for much of their time throughout the school. Regardless of whether a school today is large or small, headteachers must now regard themselves primarily as managers. They are now called upon to monitor the totality of financial management: the setting and the oversight of the school budget, the costing of staff, the maintenance of buildings and grounds, the creation and payment of invoices and the ability to read spreadsheets. This consequently took them and their deputies away from the classroom, adding a psychological pressure because many staff in these responsible posts came into school to teach and initially, at least, felt guilty because the role for which they had been trained, that of teachers of children, had been emasculated and they were now expected to be managers, with very little, and sometimes no, training.

All schools now have a fully delegated budget and have procedures and system to deal with the financial accounting necessary to ensure the smooth running of the school. Yet this was only the beginning of the change process. Headteachers and senior staff have since 1988 been through a tremendous learning curve and now have a much wider brief with great responsibility. As new government policies were introduced the plethora of documentation has continued to impact on the administration workload within the school. As each new circular has come into school so another policy has to be written. Schools now need to have a wide range of policies, as shown below. This list is extensive but not exclusive. There may be as many more policy documents as the headteacher and governors deem to be advisable.

Creating policies is not enough. Headteachers have the responsibility to ensure that they are put into practice. The only way to do this is to monitor that all policies are implemented correctly and successfully.

The range of school policies

- the delivery for all subjects of the National Curriculum
- religious education and collective worship
- behaviour and discipline
- sex education
- equal opportunities
- assessment, recording and reporting to parents
- special educational needs provision and the Code of Practice
- roles and responsibilities of the governing body
- pay and conditions of service
- charging for school activities
- admissions to school
- health and safety
- budgeting

To complete this mammoth task schools need to manage and organise this activity. They need to plan the monitoring process over a period of time, and therefore must create a monitoring programme.

Over recent years one document which has become central to the planning and organisation of schools is the school development plan. In 1989 LEAs were influenced by the then Department of Education and Science, following the publication of *Planning for School Development* (Hargreaves *et al.* 1989), to encourage schools to formulate school development plans. All schools are now required by the Office For Standards in Education (OFSTED) to provide a development plan at the time of inspection. The annual report by Her Majesty's Chief Inspector (OFSTED 1996a) states that:

> Good headteachers, supported by their governors, create a climate in which the staff (and sometimes pupils, parents and local employers) are able to reflect on current achievements in an honest and dispassionate manner . . . In the best schools this process of review is then translated into a development plan which details who is going to do what, when, how initiatives are to be funded, and how the implementation of an action is to be monitored. Effective planning of this kind is, as yet, relatively rare.
>
> (OFSTED 1996a: 11)

Hargreaves *et al.* (1989) identify four main processes in development planning:

- *Auditing*: a school reviews its strengths and weaknesses.
- *Construction planning*: a school identifies where it wants to be by a given point in time, selecting piorities for development and turning them into targets.
- *Implementation*: a school implements its planned tasks and meets its targets.
- *Evaluation*: a school checks the success of its implementation.

School development planning has assisted many schools on to the first rung of the ladder for school evaluation and improvement. The success of development planning depends on the continual involvement of and support from all staff. The best way to keep all staff committed is to involve everyone in the creation of aspects of the plan, according to their particular skills and interests. They also need to be kept informed about those aspects of the plan that other staff are responsible for, so that they take ownership of targets and tasks for the forthcoming years.

Once these goals are incorporated there comes the need to ensure that they are being delivered. This can only be done through regular monitoring. There should, therefore, be a system devised that involves all staff in examining the progress of the implementation of their targets. These can then be formally reviewed against the success criteria for each task and the evidence recorded.

Monitoring is therefore central to the planning cycle, and plans for it should be explicitly identified. It is an ongoing activity which will supply information to aid the completion of the targets of each member of staff. In schools that successfully implement development planning all staff play a vital role in the review process. These schools have provided themselves with a major ingredient of the self-monitoring school.

WHAT DO WE MONITOR?

We need to monitor everything! There is a need to monitor the implementation of policies, schemes and guidelines to ensure that the curriculum provision is broad and relevant to the needs of the pupils. The time allocation for each subject needs to be checked to ensure the delivery of a balanced curriculum. The curriculum planning and any individual education plans need to be surveyed to ensure continuity and progression and full entitlement to the National Curriculum for all pupils. All external tests need to be scrutinised and analysed so that staff can plan further development and so improve their teaching. The accuracy and consistency of teachers' assessment, including marking, should be checked to guarantee that the arrangements for assessing pupils' progress is promoting higher standards of learning.

Senior managers and subject coordinators need to observe classroom practice so that the outcomes of the whole system of the schools' planning can be monitored. Pupils' learning must be observed to see if they are making progress in knowledge, skills and understanding and that they are acquiring new concepts while they are developing the right attitude to learning. The quality of learning and standards achieved by pupils with special educational needs must be appraised to ensure that the requirements of the statements for provision are being met. An assessment must be made on how well the pupils' attainment matches their potential ability. The information gained from classroom observation will lead to an informed, whole school discussion from which targets will be set to improve teaching.

There needs to be an evaluation of the strategic management of the resources available to the school to check that staff, learning resources and accommodation are deployed to best achieve the stated aims and objectives. The financial planning needs to be monitored to ensure the effectiveness of the control procedures. The purchase and use of resources need to be overseen so as to guarantee that they are sufficient and appropriate, accessible and of good quality.

Pupils' behaviour in school should be observed and recorded to ensure that the school's arrangements for promoting good behaviour are effective. The quality of relationships should be included in this observation so that an evaluation can be made of how the school promotes pupils' moral and social development.

The school's documentation for parents, including the school prospectus, needs constantly to be checked to ensure that parents' contribution to school life is being encouraged and the quality of information provided is good and up to date.

WHO SHOULD MONITOR?

Everyone has a responsibility to monitor and everyone must be monitored. In the self-monitoring school there must be a shared philosophy, a partnership and team work. One of the main findings in the OFSTED report *Access and Achievement in Urban Education* (1993a) is that: 'monitoring and evaluation of the learning of pupils and the outcomes of teaching are weak features in many schools'.

THE OFSTED PROCESS AND SELF-REVIEW AND MONITORING

By June 1998 it is planned that all maintained primary schools in England will have been inspected under the system for inspection managed by the Office For Standards in Education (OFSTED). This body was set up by the Department for Education to replace Her Majesty's Inspectorate, which for the previous 152 years had been responsible for inspecting schools. OFSTED has, since September 1993, been responsible for implementing the Framework for Inspection, which identifies the criteria and methods for all inspections. It is interesting to note the influence that these inspections have had on schools throughout the country since the first training inspections in 1993, set up to create a new breed of inspectors, mainly LEA inspectors or advisers or retired HMI. These inspectors were to lead and recruit teams of private inspectors, who were to tender for the inspection of schools. HMI were brought in to mentor and train the new inspectors, who were using for the first time the newly created *Framework for Inspection*. This was a traumatic period for the inspected schools which often found that they were not well prepared and did not have the documentation that was required. It was also a shock that the inspections were so thorough, with so much documentation required. Information about the inspection process was disseminated through the grapevine and schools produced the required policies, schemes and guidelines in advance of any notification of inspection. This has paid dividends and it was encouraging to find Her Majesty's Chief Inspector in the 1996 Annual Report stating that 'most schools now have a range of curriculum documentation in the form of policy statements and schemes of work' (OFSTED 1996a: 49).

Inspections are certainly influencing schools' practice and it is interesting to note that the same report, unlike its predecessors, frequently refers to monitoring (*ibid.*):

> Subject co-ordinators need more time to monitor outcomes of their planning by working alongside colleagues in the classroom ... Monitoring to see that the agreed procedures are being used and evaluation to discover their effects on the performance of pupils are poorly developed.

and again, this time as a criticism, (*ibid.*: 70):

> Many [schools] lack systems to monitor and evaluate effectively the quality of teaching and standards of achievement ... A surprising number of schools lack an effective system for budgeting and monitoring expenditure.

There is no doubt, therefore, that schools are now being encouraged even more systematically to monitor and observe how curriculum and pedagogic initiatives affect pupil learning. It has been stated earlier in this chapter, but needs reiterating, that monitoring is a continuous process of examining and observing. It is part of self-review which states where we are, but it is also checking that we are on the path to where we want to be.

There have, in the past, been other approaches to school review and one that has been used successfully is the Guidelines for the Review and Internal Development of Schools, known by the acronym GRIDS (Abbott *et al.* 1988). This consists of individual survey sheets completed by all staff, which school coordinators then analyse. The results are then presented to the staff and, corporately, an area for specific review is selected. This scheme, and many like it, will no doubt in the future still be used, but the OFSTED *Framework for Inspection* will also serve as a basis for creating a self-review model.

The inspection process

The *Framework for Inspection* is a comprehensive set of criteria against which schools are inspected, by teams of independent inspectors, which include a lay inspector and is led by a Registered Inspector. The purpose of the inspection is to improve the quality of education, to raise standards by identifying strengths and weaknesses in schools. The inspection judges a school to be effective according to its success in relation to the following aspects of its work:

- the quality of education provided by the school
- whether the financial resources made available to the school are managed efficiently
- the spiritual, moral and social and cultural development of pupils at the school.

(OFSTED 1995a: 8)

Before the inspection

From the notification by OFSTED that a school is to be inspected, the governors and headteacher have three weeks to complete and return Form S. This form gives a detailed specification which constitutes the basis of the information which is put out in the tender. Registered Inspectors (RGIs) apply to secure the contract for inspection through a bidding process. Once the contract has been agreed, the RGI will then contact the school and agree dates for the beginning and end of the inspection. The school will then be visited by the lead inspector to discuss the purpose of the inspection and negotiate a programme with the head-teacher and the governors. It is at this point that the school will be informed about the required documentation that is listed in the OFSTED *Handbook* 1996.

The RGI, during the initial visit to the school, will discuss the inspection process and provide information about the composition of the team. The required documentation includes:

- samples of pupils' work
- records and reports
- teachers' planning
- any guidelines, policies or schemes of work available
- individual education plans
- timetables

This will be collected and any other information that the school may choose to make available during the inspection week will be discussed. The school's documentation will then be scrutinised by the inspection team who will prepare and share a 'background information report' on the school.

Before the inspection begins the RGI has to hold a pre-inspection parents' meeting where the purpose and process of the inspection will be explained. Parents at that meeting and through a questionnaire will be invited to pass comments on these issues (OFSTED 1995b: 26):

- pupils' progress and standards of work
- the part parents play in the life of the school
- the information which the school provides for parents
- the help and guidance available to pupils

- the values which the school teaches
- homework
- behaviour and attendance

During the inspection

The main activity during the inspection week is to gather evidence on which the judgments of the team are based from:

- observation of lessons and other activities
- scrutiny of a representative sample of pupils' work
- discussions with staff and governors
- scrutiny of a range of documentation to include policies, schemes and guidelines and teachers' planning
- observation of work displayed in hall corridors and classrooms

During the inspection week the team will meet regularly to arrive at corporate judgments on the responses to their criteria and, in particular, to assess how well the school is led and how efficiently the school is managed. Teachers with managerial and curricular responsibilities will meet with the appropriate inspector and will receive an oral feedback on inspection findings.

After the inspection

The headteacher and the governors will have the opportunity, separately, to discuss the inspection findings with the RGI. These meetings are held prior to the written report being finalised. Judgments will not be changed but these meetings give the staff and governors the opportunity to correct any factual errors. The report is then written in such a way as to give to the parents and the local community a clear understanding of the school's strengths and weaknesses.

Action planning

When the report is received, the school governors and staff have to respond to the findings of the inspection and review established priorities in the form of an action plan. This has to be created within forty days of receipt of the report. The best plans are drawn up consultatively by governors, the headteacher and staff, and incorporate:

- specific targets for raising standards or improving quality of provision
- practical strategies and programmes of development focused on these goals

- arrangements for monitoring and evaluating the progress and impact of the measures taken

(OFSTED 1995a: 3)

The inspection report on a school, together with the school's own self-assessment, will help the key personnel to build up a profile of the quality of educational provision, the outcomes, the standards and achievements of the students, both academically and socially. The strengths and the weaknesses of the policies, procedures and practices will become apparent, together with the effectiveness of the management systems and structures. From this clear analysis schools and governors have a basis on which to plan their development. They can identify where they need to take remedial action, where they can plan for progressive improvement and where they can celebrate success. This is the beginning of their analysis of the whole-school approach to their educational provision.

INSPECTION AND SELF-REVIEW

Inspections are a thorough, external review of the whole school system. There are many opportunities for schools to use this inspection system to their advantage; in fact schools can use the impetus of external reform for internal purposes (Hopkins *et al.* 1994). In the preliminary period, the preparation of the relevant documentation gives senior managers, staff and governors an overview of all their policies and procedures. They can begin to evaluate where they are in relation to the framework requirements.

The advantage of using the inspection process to aid self-review is that procedures are well documented in the *Framework for Inspection*. This documentation is a comprehensive set of criteria against which schools can monitor, self-assess and audit. It can be used as the basis for creating procedures and these will form a policy for monitoring. A study of the *Framework* will give schools a list of the policies and practices that need to be regularly checked.

The monitoring of teachers' planning, classroom delivery and children's learning, as matched to the *Framework*, leads to reflection on practice, informed discussion on teaching and learning strategies, and in turn to the planned improvement of curriculum content and delivery. This is the beginning of the analysis of the whole-school approach to the educational provision in the school.

A major shift of approach by OFSTED now allows schools to supply 'other information the school wishes to be considered, including any documentations about, and the outcomes of any school evaluation activities' (OFSTED 1996b: 22). This is an encouragement for schools to become self-reviewing institutions. It is also a recognition that the OFSTED inspection is part of a continuum of progressive improvement. The *Framework* provides the criteria against which schools are measured, but it is also a standard for which to aim.

Chapter 2

The management of monitoring

Grahame Robertson

Grahame Robertson qualified as a teacher in 1971 at Dudley College of Education and obtained his B.Phil. (Ed.) in 1988 at Birmingham University. As senior master at Kates Hill he gained experience of education management, including the introduction of school monitoring processes. This duality of interest prompted him to write this chapter. He is now deputy head in Highgate Primary School, Dudley.

The Oxford English Dictionary defines ethos as the 'characteristic spirit of community, people, or system' and in order for an effective monitoring policy and system to operate within a school it is vital that a special 'spirit' is created and maintained. What that spirit is, how it can be created in a way which will motivate and inspire a staff, and how it can grow and strengthen are abstract questions which need considerable thought and discussion. It may be that there are no specific answers to them, and a discussion in this chapter may not be able to offer advice or guidance on creating such an ethos. However, discussion may clarify the kind of vision that a manager or group of managers needs to have in order to make possible monitoring systems which staff respect and value.

In the typical mid-twentieth-century pre-National Curriculum primary school, where a paternalistic/autocratic type of management style was prevalent, the ethos was created almost totally by the headteacher. Staff respected the traditional headship role and generally accepted that their leader was a guide and protector. The headteacher led and managed all areas of school organisation: administration; recruiting staff; coordinating curriculum planning; being an exemplar of the moral, social and aesthetic curriculum; disciplining the children, dealing with parents and nurturing the staff. The ethos within this model was a static concept, based on long-held traditions. The selective secondary education system with the 11+ examination assessing which children should go to grammar and which to secondary modern schools created a model for primary schools and provided a set of performance indicators based on the children's success in the examination. Year groups were usually streamed and the children in the top groupings were often groomed for success. In this period, evaluation in schools was based on the children's ability, and the skills of the teachers in delivering knowledge were accepted as part of their training and professionalism. Individual child failure was most often seen as the result of poor intellect.

Monitoring undoubtedly took place in schools, as it was accepted that the headteacher was responsible for ensuring that the delivery of knowledge was taking place throughout the school. As the headteacher was often involved in the tutoring of the upper streams there was respect by the staff for the excellent practitioner and the ultimate monitor. Where the headteacher's style was paternalistic the staff would almost certainly have regarded regular visits to their classrooms as supportive and helpful, whilst the more autocratic style would have created a greater sense of being 'checked'. Either way this process of monitoring was accepted as part of the headteacher's daily work and, by its nature, would not have been particularly threatening to the teaching staff.

The accent on accountability in these schools was very different from that of the 1990s. In most schools teachers with curriculum responsibility posts wrote schemes of work for their colleagues to follow, headteachers expected a regular written forecast or report about knowledge being delivered and, occasionally, an LEA adviser would visit the school to look at a particular area. It was not part of the curriculum postholder's contractual role to ensure that the schemes of work were properly delivered in the classroom. Headteachers generally relied on the professionalism of their staff and signed the weekly forecasts after briefly reading them through, and the LEA adviser might make positive suggestions to the headteacher, to aid development and improvement. Very occasionally a team of Her Majesty's Inspectorate (HMI) visited a school for several days to make a thorough assessment of the school, reporting back confidentially and, largely, developmentally. Most teachers would have seen their career through without such an inspection.

Years of this generally unquestioned respect and faith in the profession led to a general attitude that to question or scrutinise the work of teachers was unacceptable. Moreover, the ethos of the primary school was built on the headteacher's belief that the staff were the deliverers of knowledge to the children, trusted always to do that effectively, and respected by parents and society.

In 1983 James Callaghan delivered his famous speech at Ruskin College suggesting that we needed measures to ensure the quality of our teachers. As a direct result of his suggestions, though much later, the concept of regular teacher appraisal was introduced. Initially it met with powerful resistance from a large majority of teachers and their professional bodies, but a national steering group representative of teacher unions and associations, LEAs, the DES and HMI produced a definitive report entitled

School Teacher Appraisal: a National Framework (HMSO 1989). It was still to be a further two years before regulations were laid before Parliament (Poster and Poster 1993). For the first time since the days of 'payment by results' teachers were to have their work monitored.

When the 1988 Education Reform Act (ERA) introduced a National Curriculum into the English and Welsh systems a new kind of account-ability was imposed on our schools, and the kind of ethos described earlier could not easily survive. Teachers now had to deliver a set programme of learning, ensure that children gained an 'entitlement' of education, and demonstrate that they had achieved this through assessments and evidence. More recently, the setting up of the Office For Standards in Education (OFSTED) with its programme of stringent school inspections, has given even more strength to the government's process of school evaluation and assessment of the quality of teaching and learning. At the end of the twentieth century and into the twenty-first, teachers may continue to feel threatened and vulnerable, but equally important to their personal concerns is the need for our schools to raise standards and improve quality.

Faced with the demands of the National Curriculum and impending OFSTED inspection, a school staff needs to be very carefully managed into the process of self-monitoring, and a very different ethos needs to be created from that of previous eras. Barton *et al.* (1980: 103), writing about accountability in education, point out that:

> Any programme of public accountability – of maintaining confidence by the application of recognized routines for monitoring standards and solving problems – would be hopelessly precarious in the absence of any mutual sense of trust.

The mutual trust discussed here refers primarily to that required between parents and schools in addressing the question of accountability in the wider community. However, this can be applied to the successful introduction of curriculum monitoring systems in a school which requires an equally firm foundation of trust between the staff, who will eventually be both monitors and those monitored.

SCHOOL ORGANISATION AND MANAGEMENT STYLES

School management studies published over the past fifty years describe a variety of management theories and styles which try to assess the most effective environments within which good teaching and learning can take place. Several modern theorists describe existing theories within five broad perspectives categorised by Bush *et al.* (1990: 12–25): the bureaucratic, collegial, political, subjective and ambiguity perspectives.

The bureaucratic model is based on the work of Weber (1947), but still holds true for many late twentieth-century institutions. It is a hierarchical model which advocates clear-cut divisions of labour. A school operating in this way will have a hierarchical authority structure and a very clear system of rules and regulations. A major criticism of this model is that it neglects the individual qualities of staff, and regards them as cogs in the organisational wheel, there to implement the systems and rules through their own professional skills and knowledge, but with limited influence.

The collegial or democratic model acknowledges the vital role of professional personnel in the management of the organisation. Hierarchical structures are minimised, and decisions are arrived at through discussion and consensus. Bush (Bush *et al.* 1990: 14) writes:

> In its pure form all members of the collegium have an equal opportunity to influence policies. Decisions emerge through a process of discussion leading to consensus. Staff are thought to hold a common set of values that underpin the decision-making process and lead to shared institutional aims.

In the political perspective, conflict is a major feature of an organisation's management, with decisions being arrived at after a process of bargaining and negotiation, where the relative power of the people involved is crucial to the outcomes. The theory accepts that conflict is a natural feature of any organisation, and effective management is about the skilful resolution and, possibly, manipulation of this conflict.

Subjective perspectives are quite different from the other management models described by the theorists, in that they assert the importance of the individual within an organisation, rather than the whole. These perspectives suggest that all individuals hold their own beliefs about the organisation's ethos, purposes and goals. Events and associated decision making may be interpreted in many different ways according to people's beliefs and perceptions. Here, the clear-cut and strictly set structure of the bureaucratic models gives way to the beliefs and attitudes of individual people. Greenfield (1973) maintains that no organisational structure can be independent of the people within it and assures us that 'individuals not only create the organisation, they are the organisation'.

The final models are termed ambiguity perspectives, and these hinge on the constant change and flux that takes place within an organisation. Institutional aims and goals are unclear, and decision making follows a complex pattern of participation by different people in different degrees, according to the nature of the decision: hence the concept of ambiguity. In their American research, Cohen *et al.* (1972) describe a 'garbage can' into which personnel throw problems and solutions, and decisions are the result of a mixture of influences from different people, circumstances and choices. March (1974: 30), analysing ambiguity, explains his belief that:

Our usual management recommendations are classic: If you do not know what your objectives are, take the time to identify them. If you do not know what your alternatives are, search and you will find them. If you do not understand your technology, undertake research . . . to establish the cause-and-effect connections in your activities. Such recommendations are not wrong; but they are frequently inadequate . . . The idea of establishing goals first and then acting has some limitations as a model behaviour.

Other theorists approach their studies of school management from different perspectives. Nias (1980), for example, studied primary school headteacher leadership styles and types, rather than the style of the organisation as a whole. She describes three styles of leadership: passive, positive and Bourbon. She asserts her belief in the power that these individuals can wield over the management of primary schools, and the effects that this can have on the job satisfaction of personnel.

The passive leader sets a low professional standard and has a low level of personal involvement in school. No monitoring of teacher standards takes place and the administration systems are weak. This type of leader is hard to pin down for any discussion on issues, gives little support to individual teachers, and has no perceived aims. In her research Nias found that teachers did not favour this kind of leader:

They perceived themselves as totally free to set their own goals, under headteachers whose professional standards did not match their own, and who offered neither coherence to the school as a whole nor support and guidance to individuals.

(Nias 1980: 261)

Positive leaders set high professional standards and are highly personally involved in the school. They make themselves available for discussion and show concern for teacher morale and individual development. Leadership is strong in setting aims for the school, and staff are encouraged to be involved in goal setting and decision making. This style of leadership was very popular in Nias' studies. Such a person 'adopted a dynamic, but consultative policy towards decision making, and actively supported the professional development of individuals' (*ibid.*).

The third style, and one which was not at all popular with the teachers in the study, is the Bourbon type. Easily described through its lack of democratic features, it presents a very inefficient administration, it treats individual teachers as inferiors, and it positively discourages (to the point of not allowing) participation in goal setting and decision making: 'the "Bourbon" was characterised by social distance, authoritarian professional relationships, and administrative inefficiency' (*ibid.*)

None of these theories exists in its purest form, and the reader will recognise facets of each one within organisations they have known. Each has its positive and negative features, and to generalise about any system and say that it is 'bad' is dangerous. One can find examples of schools run by very autocratic/bureaucratic regimes which have been equally as successful, in terms of educational outcomes, as the most democratic/collegially run schools. This brief résumé of these theories will allow the readers to assess how their organisation works, and look at their own management style, to consider how these can affect decision making, and affect the way forward in successfully introducing self-monitoring procedures.

Because of the very sensitive nature of teachers monitoring each other's work, especially inside the classroom, it is unlikely that a strongly autocratic regime, imposing narrow and mechanistic systems, will avoid high levels of stress and friction. An overall judgment may be that more democratic, collegial relationships, where planning, delivering and assessing the curriculum are shared, will lend themselves more easily to the introduction of school monitoring systems, with all the challenges they bring.

CREATING THE ETHOS FOR MONITORING

It is imperative that readers look at the implementation of monitoring within the structure of their own schools, and the range of personalities within that structure. Monitoring is fundamentally a developmental process, and a school which is used to a maintenance working mode, with a reactive, rather than pro-active style, will probably need to develop a new, more dynamic approach. The path must be trodden with circumspection, and figure 2.1 on page 35 is a list of issues which it may be useful for the reader to address with colleagues, with a view to building developmental processes, where it is felt necessary.

Having raised these questions it may be helpful to address them, and consider the approaches of staff in some schools where monitoring systems have recently been implemented.

UNDERSTANDING THE MANAGEMENT

One school with a headteacher committed to ensuring the efficiency of the management structure on her appointment immediately set about restructuring, as it was obvious that the existing set-up was inappropriate to the school's newly devised aims, objectives and ethos. All meetings now follow the pattern in figure 2.2 on page 36.

This process extends into all activities in the school, especially in classrooms where the best lesson planning and delivery depends on the

Plan–Do–Review approach. There is a history of collegial approaches to all aspects of planning and decision making, and a high degree of delegation to individuals and groups has created a confident and developed team of professionals. These attributes would benefit any school venturing into the monitoring process.

With the introduction of the National Curriculum, and the delegation of finance to schools, this headteacher soon became aware of the changing roles of headteachers and deputies. Management structures were designed to create mutually supportive teams to share many of the responsibilities which had traditionally been held by the headteacher and deputy.

This did not herald the negation of responsibilities by the most senior staff and, at all stages of delegation, the headteacher and deputy had overall line management responsibility for the tasks and projects of the moment. Staff soon felt the benefits of team working, both in and out of the classrooms, and their self-esteem grew in the knowledge that they were more closely involved with the management of the school. The most important example of this commitment to whole-staff involvement is the annual production of the school development/business plan, where all staff, teaching and non-teaching, have the opportunity to input their ideas to the planning for the following twelve months. Once, it was quite common to hear teachers say: 'I wish I could have more management responsibility!', but this is no longer so. It is very important to help teachers understand that there are few management roles more demanding than those required to run an efficient classroom: administration, planning, delivering, personnel, time-management, assessment, reporting, to name but a few. Helping teachers to see themselves as developing managers from the earliest part of their career, and then extending this into their work with colleagues outside the classroom, has been a very powerful force in this school, and one which helped the headteacher to move successfully towards a monitoring policy.

A quality system, following the pattern of Plan–Do–Review, has developed which requires reports to be completed by staff at all levels of the structure, indicating timescales, aims and objectives, tasks to be completed, resources required, and reviews. These have to be given at stated times to line managers who are thus able to monitor the progression of projects and developments across the school. This system took time to develop and, again, involved everyone in writing procedures which they felt were appropriate and relevant, but did not create paperwork for its own sake.

This school has very successfully addressed the issues of creating clear and effective procedures to ensure that responsibilities are met, and has developed noticeably open channels of communications. It would be false to suggest that, when the time came for the school to ask the question: 'Are we ready to observe, and be observed by others?', there was total confidence about the outcomes. There is no doubt that the management approaches and systems described in this section created an ethos that eliminated feelings of dread when the question of monitoring was first broached.

UNDERSTANDING THE CURRICULUM

Before any monitoring can take place, the foundations of an effective curriculum need to be firmly built. This does not mean that every area of every subject will be totally in order, and in a dynamic organisation this should never be the case, since it implies that a state of sterility has been reached. OFSTED inspectors are looking for evidence that the curriculum is being regularly audited and reviewed, and that areas of documentation, implementation, resourcing and evaluation are being properly planned for. They will not be impressed by a library of documents which are not transferred into practice within the school.

In order for staff to share the new levels of accountability that recent legislation has incurred, the headteacher of this school decided to use all above-scale points for wider management roles, rather than for individual subject coordination. There is an overall curriculum coordinator with three accompanying posts overseeing the core and foundation subjects. All other teachers have a specific subject to coordinate in line with national recommendations that every teacher should have a curriculum management role and, ultimately, a monitoring role. This organisation has achieved a deeper awareness of the accountability that the whole staff share for the provision for all pupils of a broad, balanced and well differentiated curriculum.

Obviously it is not easy for schools to make radical changes of this kind, if their above-scale points are already designated for existing subject roles and role-shift is difficult to accomplish. However, creating strategies to ensure that all teachers have a role to play in managing part of the curriculum will help to raise awareness of their new accountability. They will need to support an existing coordinator and perhaps take on an area of development within the subject brief.

In smaller schools, where staff have been obliged for many years to shoulder the responsibility of not one, but several curriculum areas, any exercise for raising accountability awareness will hardly be necessary, but it may be possible here to engineer a higher level of team work, to give each other greater support. Policies, guidelines and schemes will then develop from shared understandings, and with shared work loads. Any school, whatever its size or stage of development, can audit the curriculum, decide what needs to be done, draw up an action plan to prioritise tasks and indicate how and when the development work is going to be done. Meeting times will need to be earmarked for the work, and a systematic schedule agreed to complete each task. A small primary school has taken this approach, and the stress levels which existed previously due to the heavy burdens on staff have been greatly reduced. The teachers have developed a much wider understanding of their school's curriculum because of the collegial approach to planning it and writing their documentation. The headteacher is committed to involving as many outside agencies as possible within the school; and, as each area of the curriculum has been audited, the relevant LEA advisory staff have been asked to take a major role in guiding the work. LEA advisers can be an important resource. Once a firm curriculum foundation is in place the need for monitoring and the criteria to guide it begin to become clearer.

STRIVING FOR IMPROVEMENT

The school in which I was until recently a senior member of staff is in an inner-town area with considerable levels of social and educational deprivation. Such schools are all too readily described as 'failing schools' because their academic achievements are compared with those of schools in greener pastures.

Since the introduction of the National Curriculum, the staff have addressed assessment issues in their long-term, medium-term and short-term curriculum planning systems. The pupils are thoroughly 'baselined' when they come into school to record their basic skills and knowledge, and teachers routinely use assessment tasks to measure achievement and improvement. Only through such procedures can evidence of the value-added factor be shown.

The school's fine-tuned planning and assessment procedures are now at the heart of the self-monitoring for quality explained in detail in chapter 4. What followed the introduction of this was an understanding by class teachers and curriculum coordinators in particular of the need to improve standards of teaching and learning. The question was posed: 'We have developed excellent documentation and procedures to monitor our written plans. How can we make sure that the material we plan to teach is properly delivered and effectively learnt?'

Discussion involving the whole staff led to a decision to pilot a classroom monitoring system. It must be said that, at this time, the staff were not sure that they were completely ready to accept the possible threats involved in monitoring and being monitored. Readers would be well advised to spend time thinking through the outcomes of teachers becoming critical of each others' practice. Staff from this school, who now front INSET programmes for schools across the Midlands, involve course members in role play situations to address the feedback process from classroom observations. Generally, teachers are by nature considerate and caring people: these are qualities which draw them to working with children in the first place, and they are evident in the difficulty that the majority of teachers have in understanding both the need for and the parameters of the delivery of professional criticism to colleagues. Readers attempting the introduction of monitoring must address these difficulties, and the success of the process will hinge quite dramatically on the state of morale in the school.

POSITIVE MORALE

This school has a history of strong staff development procedures. In the late 1980s, when national teacher appraisal was being regarded with suspicion and distrust, the headteacher, along with colleague headteachers, was contributing to the design of an appraisal process which was totally developmental. Staff look forward to their appraisals to gain support in areas of their work they want to develop, and for opportunities to make reciprocal observations about the development of the school. As well as the annual appraisal interview, all members of staff have a meeting with the school's staff development officer to discuss their own management, curriculum and career needs. The details gleaned from both interviews feed back into the planning process for personal and professional development, and inform the in-service training programme.

The developmental appraisal process in this school has nurtured a concern for self-improvement, and teachers see the personal benefits which can be gained by honing their management and teaching skills. It was at this stage that the headteacher asked the staff: 'Are we ready to write a monitoring policy?' They responded positively, even enthusiastically, though they were well aware that there was much hard work involved.

MAKING A START

There can be no more useful starting point for discussions about monitoring than the OFSTED *Framework for the Inspection of Schools* (1995a), because it provides a set of criteria against which to measure success. Whether or not we agree with the current process of inspection is not important: the criteria on which classrooms are being viewed are generally accepted as being valuable and relevant. While an imminent inspection should not be the main driving force to make a school more aware of its development and improvement, it can create a positive motivation in those schools where maintenance management is prevalent. A danger here though, is that it may lead to panic, through a sudden realisation that perhaps more developmental work should have gone on in the past. Some headteachers and their management teams have traumatised their teachers by suddenly announcing the need for policies, guidelines, schemes of work, forecasts and more, within a very short timescale. This is not the kind of ambience whereby the OFSTED requirements for documentation will be met in a constructive way, with systems designed to bring true development within a stable environment.

In a school where teachers are used to the introduction of developmental initiatives, and have become less overwhelmed by the steep learning curves caused by imposed change, the introduction of self-monitoring will be easier. This initiative demands a sensitive approach, one which must build high levels of mutual trust and understanding. Within any school, for an initiative to work, there must be a strong commitment and belief in its value by those in major leadership roles. Whether the headteacher makes a unilateral decision to introduce monitoring, or a senior management team plans it before taking the decision to the staff, or the whole staff are involved from the very beginning, it is essential that there is a whole-school understanding of what the monitoring process is going to involve for everyone concerned.

Headteachers and deputies wanting to introduce monitoring systems are well placed by their position in the school management structure to stimulate other staff, and to create an atmosphere of interest. If the prospective innovator is not a member of the senior management team, but a member of staff committed to the importance of monitoring, it will be essential to sell the idea to senior colleagues, so that they can support its introduction and implementation before the whole school staff. At whatever level the reader is working, it will be beneficial to present an outline to colleagues explaining the importance of monitoring in ensuring the reality of curriculum policies, the transfer of those policies into practice, and the school's commitment to continually raising standards. Reference to figure 2.1 on page 35 will be useful to schools making a start.

APPRAISAL, MONITORING, INSPECTION

It is useful to consider how monitoring meshes with other forms of school-based assessment, namely teacher appraisal and OFSTED inspection. Figure 2.3 on page 37 shows these three elements with their particular qualities listed underneath. This has proved a useful tool to help teachers clarify the part that each plays in school evaluation. At one extreme the OFSTED inspection is about institutional accountability and is almost totally judgmental. It involves an external team inspecting schools against a set of criteria which are applied nationally, and take little account of local circumstances. There is no negotiation, the report is final and is published for national availability.

A positive appraisal system is about personal development and self-review. It is an internal, non-judgmental process with a high degree of confidentiality, designed to raise personal standards and lead to progressive improvement of individuals and, logically, the organisation. Rather than posing a threat to teachers it is seen as a very productive activity.

Monitoring is primarily about curriculum review and development, ensuring that curriculum policy transfers into practice. The first stage of this process is the monitoring of planning through the 'paper exercise', but this can only ensure that the plans meet the requirements set down in the policies, guidelines and schemes. The only sure way to see that the pupils are receiving the learning they should, in the way that they should, is through monitoring in the classroom. Clearly, monitoring teachers' work, both the planning and the teaching, has an element of threat which classroom observation within the appraisal model rarely has. On the other hand, it is not as judgmental as the process of inspection. Setting out on the path of monitoring will not be advanced by any suggestions that it will not involve criticism of the work of colleagues, though clearly this criticism must be constructive. The staff of the school in which monitoring was piloted voiced this when it was agreed that 'to have any effect monitoring must have teeth!' Their early experiences clarified the need for staff to discuss ways of managing the feedback process, to learn how to handle positive criticism, and avoid the trauma of personalising it – very easy to state, much harder to do.

MANAGING CLASSROOM OBSERVATIONS AND THE FEEDBACK PROCESS

The most sensitive stage of monitoring is at the point of classroom observation, and it is here that the most careful management of the whole process must take place. The senior staff at this school will freely observe that, in spite of spending a great deal of valuable time creating a positive ethos towards monitoring generally, they did not foresee the difficulties that would arise from observing in the classrooms and, particularly, feeding back criticisms. When the pilot monitoring programme began it was agreed that any findings from classroom observations would be fed back generally to the whole staff at a weekly staff meeting. This was done for a few weeks and no problems arose from it. However, it soon became obvious that nobody was actually taking ownership of any constructive criticisms that were being made. There was a level of denial which probably reflects a quite natural human quality, that which believes 'Unless it is aimed directly at me, I cannot take responsibility for it.' The senior staff shared these concerns with the staff, who accepted their reactions and it was agreed by consensus that, in future, the observation reports should be made to staff individually. It was at this point that the school experienced problems. The personal feedback of monitoring information to staff transported the monitors into a new world of threat and insecurity, much of which resulted from people's dislike of both giving and receiving criticism. Feelings ran so high for a time that all monitoring was stopped until the difficulties could be discussed and resolved. As soon as possible a training day was earmarked, entitled 'Monitoring: Getting It Right'. The whole staff came together to discuss the way forward in overcoming the insecurities and concerns which had surfaced during the pilot project. It was a most successful day and, in every school embarking on monitoring, staff should spend several hours discussing monitoring issues and drawing up guidelines to clarify, in everyone's mind, how classroom observations, and the feedback from them, will be managed.

The reader is able to witness one of the most valuable outcomes of the INSET day in figure 2.3 on page 37 to which reference has already been made. Coming to an understanding about where monitoring sits in terms of curriculum improvement, that is, to raise standards of teaching and learning for the pupils, and to raise teacher standards for personal development, has helped the staff to depersonalise criticisms. Now they feel less threatened about giving and receiving constructive criticism because they have a clearer understanding of the criteria for monitoring. Obviously, some have adapted more quickly than others, and the successful introduction of monitoring must take into account the different rates at which individuals take on the changes.

Role play exercises were used by staff of another school which had allocated six twilight INSET sessions to discuss the implications of classroom monitoring. They found taking on the roles of monitor and monitored very useful in breaking down some of the inhibitions teachers have in giving each other criticism. Fictional monitoring reports were written and the staff took turns at feeding back a report to a colleague, and having one fed back to them. The reports addressed some very sensitive issues and these were discussed by everyone in a plenary session at the end. Afterwards the staff felt they had developed and strengthened team building, and created new depths of understanding which would allow more mutual support and empathy.

This school had invited colleagues from a local school which had also been experimenting with monitoring, and an LEA adviser with OFSTED training and experience, to participate in the INSET meetings to share their experiences, and give advice and support. This headteacher believes strongly in not trying to reinvent the wheel, and would always advise using the services of others who have powerful experiences to share.

Having discussed the careful preparations required for classroom monitoring, figure 2.4 on page 38 provides an example of an important section of any monitoring policy, one which sets out the sequence of events. The sequence may well be adapted by other schools in the light of their own circumstances and needs.

Schools have found that the most successful classroom observations result when the observers highlighted positive aspects of the work in classrooms and picked up on a limited number of areas for constructive criticism. The complex nature of every classroom situation means that at any one time an observer could find much to criticise. The skill in monitoring is not to destroy self-esteem but to encourage teachers to be self-critical and self-improving.

MANAGING RESOURCES

These pilot schools have only been able to implement their monitoring programmes by thorough and careful planning and the deployment of the resources needed to carry them through. The staff from each school would recommend that, once the decision to implement a monitoring policy and programme has been made, short-term, medium-term and long-term plans should be formalised. As well as planning the strategies and time scales for building the right staff ethos, and getting the climate right for monitoring, important resource decisions will need to be incorporated in the school development plan.

There are primary schools where the staff, including headteacher and deputy, have a full-time teaching commitment. The opportunities for non-contact time are often non-existent, and it would be understandable for schools to feel that what has been outlined in this chapter is not feasible for them. However, there may be opportunities to introduce elements of monitoring strategies which, while they may not seem grand and extravagant, will benefit the quality of their work. Generally, it is possible for the monitoring of written planning to happen without too many resource implications. What is important here, to ensure that time resources are properly allocated, is for staff to have a clearly defined time allowance for monitoring within their contractual 1,265 working hours.

The resource implications for classroom observations are much more demanding. Senior staff need to look closely at the allocation of funds in the budget to areas which may have been crucial in the past, but may need reappraising now. An example might be that part of the budget for staff development realised through in-service courses, where there may be merit in asking the question: 'Do all the courses attended by staff provide them with sufficient insight into the organisation and delivery of the curriculum? Might school-based INSET derived from the outcomes of the self-monitoring process be more economical and at the same time more effective?' If this were found to be so, would it be feasible to transfer some of that funding towards non-contact time for subject coordinators to monitor teachers' forecasts in greater depth, or to observe in classrooms?

What matters, however, is that schools make their resource decisions – finance, time, the disposition of staff, management priorities – on the basis of regularly reviewed consideration of the needs of school, staff and pupils. There is always a danger that what was done last year, which may have seemed effective enough, will do equally well for the year to come. The self-monitoring school is better equipped to be constantly looking for better ways to approach issues both current and emergent. Using the outcomes of the self-monitoring process is the hallmark of the improving school.

Figure 2.1 Towards a monitoring process

Do we understand the management of our school?

- Are all roles clearly defined and recognised by everyone, so that staff are being used effectively?
- Are there clear, well established procedures to ensure that jobs and responsibilities are carried through?
- Are channels of communication effective and open?
- Are we ready to observe, and be observed, by others?
- Are our curriculum policies, guidelines and schemes in place?
- Is there long-, medium- and short-term planning?
- Do staff plan the curriculum collaboratively?
- Do external advisers give regular support to the process of curriculum development?
- Are the documented curriculum statements being delivered?

Are our standards improving?

- Can we improve the content of our lessons?
- Can we match work to children more precisely?
- Can we improve interest levels?

Is our morale positive?

- Do we have a good staff development policy?
- How is our appraisal process seen: as developmental, judgmental, or a procedure which we have to follow?
- Can we improve our skills and practice?
- Can monitoring help us to become more skilled, knowledgeable and mature practitioners?

Are we ready to write a monitoring policy?

Figure 2.2 The Plan–Do–Review system of management

- *Objectives and purposes are shared*: 'What do we want to achieve from the meeting?'

- *Ideas are generated* for the best way to achieve the objectives set: 'How can we do this best?' (Brainstorming is a very useful tool here.)

- *The best suggestion* is put into action. What outcomes will address the purposes set?

- *Review is carried out*: 'Have we achieved our purposes?' 'Can we improve on what we have done?'

Figure 2.3 Comparison of appraisal, monitoring, inspection

Appraisal	Monitoring	Inspection
Personal development	Curriculum development	Accountability
Self-review	Policy into practice	Spot check of quality
Internal process	*Say what you do*	Judgmental
Classroom practice	• plans and forecasts • challenge • assessment • outcomes	Raising school standards
Negotiation		Raising pupils' standards
Agreed focus	*Check that you do it*	Measuring:
Biennial	*Record findings*	• NC achievement • teaching standards • learning standards
Confidential process	*Act to:*	External agency: trained
Confidential report	• move forward • raise standards	No negotiation
Audit of INSET needs	Area or aspect specific	Four-yearly cycle
	Continuous	Institutional report
	Fast, tight feedback cycle	Published report • nationally available

Figure 2.4 A monitoring policy: timetable of events

Pre-observation meeting

- The area of monitoring is discussed and agreed.
- Specific focuses within the area are set.
- Timing of observation and follow-up meeting is decided upon.

Observation

- Depending on the focuses agreed, the monitor may sit in one place, or move around the classroom and interact with pupils and support staff.
- The monitor will use a pro-forma to write monitoring observations, and produce a written report for the teacher.

Post-observation meeting

- The monitor and teacher will discuss the observations detailed on the monitoring report.
- The monitor should strongly highlight the positive aspects of the observation.
- Constructive criticisms will be discussed, and ways of supporting the rectification or improvement of areas of practice agreed.
- All discussions will be minuted and signed. Any resource requirements, or INSET implications, will be noted and actioned by the monitor.

© 1997 Grahame Robertson

Chapter 3

Failing to plan is tantamount to planning to fail

Anna Smith

Anna Smith has had an extensive and varied career in the teaching profession spanning over twenty years. She is now in her second primary school headship. Throughout her career she has maintained a clear focus on the management of learning and the need to ensure that a suitable equilibrium is maintained between the learner, the teacher and the curriculum.

This chapter will deal with three key issues:

- *Curriculum planning*: schemes, policies and guidelines
- *Teacher planning*: long-term, medium-term and short-term
- *Monitoring of planning*

These issues will be set in the context of the importance of a whole-school approach to policy making, starting with the school development plan. This whole-school approach will be demonstrated as being effective in relation to quality assurance – in other words, how we can guarantee that:

- what we say we are providing is actually being provided
- that the provision is of high quality

The school development plan is central to the life and work of any school:

> The school through its development planning identifies relevant priorities and targets, takes the necessary action, and monitors and evaluates its progress towards them . . . school development planning is likely to be a useful process if it involves all staff productively in those elements of planning, implementation and review.
>
> (OFSTED: 1995b)

The key to a successful development plan is to have agreement on:

- the planning process itself
- the key areas for a school's development
- a structure for the plan
- the plan being viewed as an ongoing event, not a one-off document

It is not the intention of this chapter to look at the school development plan and planning process in detail. However, reference to the plan itself underpins the remainder of this chapter, and therefore the above four points need greater exposition.

THE PLANNING PROCESS

The planning process has to be cyclical in its nature, going from audit to action to review. A useful process that schools may wish to adopt is called GRASP® (Getting Results and Solving Problems). This process has four basic operations which are not hierarchical:

- Select the purpose or objective – what you want to make happen – and the criteria for success. Where are we now? Why do we want to do this? Where do we want to be? What do we want to achieve? How will we know when we have achieved it?
- Generate different ways of achieving the purpose or objective, compare with the criteria, and select the most promising. How are we going to achieve this? Have we thought of different ways? Which way will work best?
- Put the chosen plan into action and control the process. Are we committed to succeed? How will we know if we are on the right road? How will we control the course of events and keep moving in the right direction?
- Review continually and check the results. Is the purpose still valid? Are we achieving what we set out to do? Are we meeting the criteria set?

These operations can be translated into key planning processes as in figure 3.1 on page 53.

KEY AREAS FOR A SCHOOL'S DEVELOPMENT

A school can write an almost infinite number of lists of key areas for its own development, but it is advisable to focus on generic areas. The following cover the areas featured in the OFSTED framework:

- *Ethos*: school aims, spiritual, moral, social and cultural development, behaviour, pupil support, special needs, equal opportunities
- *Staffing*: management, staff development, appraisal, non-teaching/support staff
- *Curriculum*: subjects, assessment and recording
- *School community*: parents, community and business links
- *Management and organisation*: organisation of curriculum and curriculum delivery, management structure, governors
- *Resources*: material and human, building

To set priorities and targets, schools must decide whether these are innovatory or maintenance activities, that is, those which are new and those which maintain the existing developments and procedures. The result should be a balance of activities which satisfy the needs both of the organisation and of the individuals within it.

Structure for the plan

Schools must decide on their own structure. A good plan should include some or all of the following:

* school context/setting
* school aims
* innovation plans
* maintenance plans
* individual action plans
* financial costings
* appendices

The plan as an ongoing document

Schools should build into their plans times within the year when they will review the plan. Once a school has set its development plan and priorities, this will then act as a framework to control the work of the school. As the development plan will have been decided and agreed by all staff this should ensure that it will be translated into practice with commitment by all to its success and the success of the school's work.

CURRICULUM PLANNING

A weakness found to a greater or lesser degree in about three quarters of primary and middle schools is in curricular planning, and its implementation.

(DES 1985)

Building on this document the 1986 Education Act laid specific curriculum responsibilities on LEAs, governing bodies and headteachers, and in 1987 the consultation document on the National Curriculum was published. It argued that it would raise standards by 'enabling schools to be more accountable for the education they offer their pupils'. With the introduction of the National Curriculum, the concept of development planning, through the National Curriculum development plan, came into existence. In a few short years, schools were grappling with the adaptation of their own curricula to the National Curriculum, with issues related to teachers' planning and with the delivery and the concept of accountability.

It would be unfair to suggest that schools did not already have schemes in existence before the days of the National Curriculum. Most schools did have a series of schemes, in particular for areas such as mathematics and English. With the National Curriculum schools inevitably had to re-examine and audit school documents to match the requirements of the new curriculum. This led to school schemes for all National Curriculum subjects. With OFSTED came an even greater stress on school documentation. The OFSTED *Handbook of Inspection* (1993c) repeatedly mentioned three curriculum documents, namely those on policy, schemes and guidelines. The need for curriculum planning as a whole-school development galvanised the thinking of many a headteacher and senior management team.

Curriculum planning has to be built into the school development plan. It has to be an integral part of all school planning, and arguably is the most important. The curriculum impinges on resources and finances, staff training and school ethos, and therefore should not be viewed in isolation. As a school sets out its development plan, usually for the next three years, its curriculum planning should also be prioritised into the same cycle.

Just as in school development planning, schools would be wise to agree upon a process for curriculum planning. The GRASP® approach once again can provide a useful starting point for determining such a process, as figure 3.2 on page 54 shows.

If a school 'processes' three or four subjects a year through each of the key areas in figure 3.2, it will cover the whole curriculum in three years. However, a word of caution is needed: overload has to be avoided. It is for individual schools to determine their own pace according to their own circumstances. No school can write or rewrite at the same time policies, guidelines and schemes for all the National Curriculum subjects. If a school decides that there is a need for a total review of all curriculum documentation then it is crucial that this is built into the school development plan.

A total review, or even a development of curriculum documentation, is greatly enhanced by a school agreement on a common format or house style for all documentation, while acknowledging that curriculum areas have their own documentary needs. Ensuring that the terminology used in documentation is understood by all is a valuable starting point. There are three key areas for inclusion:

- *Policy*: Why are we teaching this subject?
- *Guidelines*: How are we going to teach this subject?
- *Schemes*: What are we going to teach within this subject?

POLICY

Although all curriculum documentation may be viewed by parents and governors, the policy is the only element of documentation that should be written with parents and governors being considered as the main audience, alongside teachers. The policy statement should therefore be jargon-free, written in plain English, short and to the point. Schools may wish to brainstorm their own headings for what should be contained in the policy statement, but the following list may be useful in starting that process. Each of the headings offers a sample taken from policy statements.

The nature of the subject

Religious Education within the school is an educational process, which does not seek to impose views but to explore, inform and share beliefs and practices. Religious practice is left to individual families and pupils.

School policy and the National Curriculum

Music education in school will meet the requirements of the National Curriculum and will allow children to work creatively at their own level and reach their full potential.

Curriculum aims and objectives

The school has three principal aims for religious education which reflect the Attainment targets as described in the Agreed Syllabus and also the aims of the school in its commitment to whole-child development. These are:

- to develop pupil's knowledge and understanding of religious beliefs and practices
- to help children to develop their own religious beliefs while respecting the freedom of others to hold different beliefs
- to develop the children's awareness of life experiences and the questions they raise

Approaches to teaching and learning (mathematics)

Each class teacher is responsible for the delivery of mathematics. Within the classroom the teacher should strive to provide a stimulating environment . . . Children should experience a range of teaching and learning styles and the chance to record their work in a variety of ways. Throughout the year children should have the opportunity to work either individually, with a partner or in a group. The teacher should aim to raise the status of Mathematics work highlighting what is being taught.

Points related to equality of opportunity, resources, assessment and recording, role of coordinator and staff development may also be considered as elements for inclusion in the policy. Figure 3.3 on page 55 demonstrates a complete policy statement for geography.

GUIDELINES

The guidelines element of documentation should deal with the practical issues of 'how are we going to teach the subject?' A useful tip is to write them as for newly qualified teachers joining a school staff; what will they need to know in order to teach the subject? Again, the following list is neither exhaustive nor definitive, but may assist in starting to consider the content of guidelines.

The subject: an illustration from music

Pupils should learn to understand music by:

- *Listening* to many types
- *Composing* in many styles
- *Performing* their own music, others' music
- *Appraising* music they hear

Children should learn to express their feelings and emotions through music and actually experience music appreciation as the gaining of concepts and skills is impossible at second hand. However, the elements of listening, composing, performing and appraising should not be taught separately but combined as much as possible and linked to topic work where appropriate.

Resources: illustration from religious education

Books, bibles and videos are stored in the RE cupboard in the resources room. Artefacts, photopacks and posters from the principal religions are stored in the resources room. A detailed list is kept by the RE coordinator. All resources are available to staff through a loaning system whereby the teachers signs in and out all resources. The RE coordinator has an annual budget with which to maintain and update resources. Any staff requirements should be made known to the coordinator.

Approaches to teaching and learning: illustration from science

To ensure that the aims of the science policy are achieved, a balance and variety of teaching methods should be used:

- *Class lessons*: including demonstrations
- *Project work*: individual, group and class-based
- *Practical investigations*: individual, group, class circus of activities
- *Audio-visual aids*: TV, radio, film, slides, photographs
- *fieldwork/visits*: to see real situations and events
- *visitors*: to give demonstrations/talks

Special educational needs provision

Differentiated learning is to be provided to accommodate children with special educational needs. This may take a variety of forms: by task, outcome, review, support and guidance, and intervention. Differentiation is to be specified in teachers' weekly planning forecasts.

Points related to subject specific procedures, pupils' presentation, time allocations, equal opportunities, assessment and recording and planning procedures may also be included in this section of school documentation.

Geography provision

A compete set of guidelines for geography are to be found in figure 3.4 on pages 56–7.

SCHEMES

The scheme of work is probably the most important document. It should inform teachers on the content of the subject area, and how that content is applied across the whole school. It should be written in sufficient depth and detail to allow teachers to know exactly the knowledge, skills and understanding that they must teach within the subject area. Teachers should be able to refer to what has been taught before and what will be taught after their own input. It is crucial therefore that progression and continuity is built into the scheme.

The scheme must take account of the National Curriculum and reflect its requirements; and the school's own philosophies and requirements must be taken into consideration. As the scheme of work will provide the basis for teacher planning it should be easily accessible and simple to read. Commonality of layout should be agreed as far as is possible, given that different subjects will have their own requirements. At the outset, whether curriculum documentation needs a total revamp or a planned review, schools need not only to plan this into their school development plan, but also to decide on how they are going to do this and who is going to do it. Two methods are most commonly used:

- The curriculum coordinator takes full responsibility for the whole process from audit through to dissemination to the whole staff.
- A team of people, representing all phases of the school, led by the curriculum coordinator, takes on the responsibility for the process.

It is for schools to decide the method that will work for them. The advantages and disadvantages shown in figures 3.5A and 3.5B on page 58 will assist staff to decide.

A school's curriculum documentation in the form of policies, guidelines and schemes is the essential starting point for assuring quality in curriculum delivery and practice. The curriculum is at the heart of any school. It is its translation into teaching and learning that raises the quality of experiences and standards.

Agreement on and standardisation of document layout, format and content through a planned audit, implementation and review are essential prerequisites to a school developing its monitoring and evaluation systems. A school will monitor its curriculum planning and practice against the advice it has given itself in the form of its curriculum documentation.

The documentation is translated into classroom practice through teachers planning to deliver or being prepared and then delivering or putting planning into practice. Planning processes need also to be standardised in terms of format and content for the purposes of whole-school unity and uniformity and to aid the monitoring process. The same message that has run through this chapter needs to be repeated. Changes to, or new development of planning formats and procedures need to be handled sensitively and again planned for in the school development plan. There should be whole-school involvement in examining the issues, trialing the formats and reviewing existing structures, together with discussions on planning records being available for others to monitor. If a school intends to move into a development such as monitoring of planning and practice it would be wise to enter into this with the full involvement and understanding of all staff. Discussions should begin when the development is introduced at the school development planning stage, as its implications are far reaching and can touch on issues of real professionalism.

As for standardisation of planning format and content, schools need to examine what already exists, how it meets the needs of individuals and the school and what is done with planning. The prompt questions in figure 3.6 on page 59 will aid the process.

TEACHER PLANNING

There are three stages of planning:

- *Long-term*: planning for the year
- *Medium-term*: planning for the term or half-year
- *Short-term*: planning for the week or day

Long-term

It may be in some schools that each scheme is sufficient to act as a long-term plan, especially where they have divided their schemes into individual year groups. Other schools have a discrete procedure for long-term planning, separate from the scheme. Here the scheme is used as a resource base providing information for the year plan. The advantages of a year plan are that, provided information and content are brief, then monitoring becomes an easy and quick activity:

- The subject coordinator can see at a glance whether the scheme is being followed and that all areas are covered.
- A Key Stage coordinator or resource manager can use everyone's year plan to see if there will be problems with resources.
- The teacher can ensure that all areas that need to be covered have been: for example, all four attainment targets in mathematics have been taught.
- Where teachers choose to block time, it is easier to do so with a whole year's plan.

If a school decides to follow this route then the key to success is agreement on format, but more importantly on content. If content is left to the professional judgment of individuals then there is a danger of too many levels of planning with excessively detailed content inevitably leading to problems with manageability.

Medium-term

Schools again need to agree the format and content. They may wish to consider the following as they debate medium-term planning issues:

- the knowledge, skills and understanding to be taught
- assessment opportunities
- teaching and learning activities
- time available
- resources

This list should be considered bearing in mind the key questions posed earlier:

- What is the purpose of planning?
- Who are we planning for?
- What should be in the plan?

A format which is easy to read and accessible to all should be developed: a matrix arrangement is useful and meets these criteria.

The weekly plan will probably be the object of most discussion in the staffroom, and there is no one way that will suit each and every school. Formats need to be trialed and reviewed and even once agreed upon need to be reviewed annually to ensure that they are meeting their required purpose. Considerations that need to be taken seriously at the developmental stage include:

- manageability for those writing weekly plans
- accessibility and ease of reading for those reading or monitoring weekly plans
- cost and storage of paper and photocopying
- time it takes to write, to read, to monitor, to photocopy, to file

If the planning is to be used as the first stage of monitoring curriculum policy into practice then the following elements should be considered as worthy of inclusion in the weekly plan:

- learning purpose of each lesson or sequence of lessons
- attainment targets/units/levels to be covered in each sequence of lessons
- tasks and activities children will undertake
- groupings of children
- differentiation and assessment
- review of lessons
- timing/length of lessons

As this level of planning is so crucial, some schools may wish to embark on staff development work around the areas featured in the weekly plan: for example, differentiation or clarity of learning purposes.

Once formats and contents have been agreed, schools need to consider who does the planning, when it is done and what is done with it beyond assisting the class teacher to be prepared. There are no easy answers and schools' own circumstances will influence decisions. The following is a range of possibilities:

Who plans?

- Individual teachers do all of their own planning.
- Year group teachers plan together, sharing the load of all the planning.
- Within a Key Stage or phase, one teacher plans for one curriculum area for the whole phase, a second teacher for another curriculum area and so on.
- The curriculum coordinator completes long-term and medium-term plans for his or her subject area for the whole school and then individual teachers organise their weekly plans from them.
- Any of the above with the curriculum coordinator acting as consultant.

When is planning done?

- All planning is completed in the individual's own time.
- Directed time is specifically set aside for long-term and medium-term planning, for example, the equivalent of two staff meetings per term set aside to complete termly plans, with part of an INSET day held in the summer term for long-term planning.

What is done with planning?

- Is it for the teacher's use alone?
- Is planning submitted to the headteacher only?
- Is planning monitored by a variety of people, for example, curriculum coordinators, phase leaders, senior management team?

If a school is interested in being reflective of its own practice, in raising standards as a result of that reflection and of assuring quality of its curriculum planning and delivery, then the last strategy is probably the best way forward.

THE MONITORING OF PLANNING

This is the first step along the road of quality assurance, provided that a whole-school approach to policy and documentation has been undertaken. The correct ethos for monitoring, and an understanding of and a sharing in the development of monitoring across a school are essential for it to succeed. Equally, consideration must be given as to who will monitor, what will be monitored, when the monitoring will take place and the nature of the feedback given. These issues must be planned for at the inception of the development and must be included in the school development plan.

What follows is a description of one school's attempts at monitoring its curriculum planning as a precursor to monitoring classroom practice. Chapter 4 will focus in greater detail on this issue.

The tradition in the school was that of the headteacher and/or deputy headteacher monitoring all the school planning. The monitoring of planning and practice as a whole-school issue was in the school development plan and INSET time was set aside to discuss this development. It was agreed to focus on the monitoring of planning first, and discussions and deliberations and the formulation of procedures and formats took place throughout two terms, by whole-staff and senior management teams as appropriate. During the third term agreement was reached on procedures and formats, and a start date of the new school year.

INSET for communication and negotiation skills was provided to all staff during the third term. It was agreed that all curriculum coordinators would monitor the yearly and termly plans using the formats and agreed criteria for monitoring each level of planning.

Yearly plan

This included the coverage of attainment targets and units. The scheme and resource implications and continuity and progression across year groups were also part of the plan. The focus for coordinators was to ensure that for each class or year group all attainment targets and units were covered throughout the year, and that the school scheme was being followed. It was imperative that for the school as a whole there would be no extra resource implications or clashes and that there was progression and continuity across year groups.

Termly plan

The focus for termly monitoring was to ensure that what had been planned for on the yearly plan was followed through in termly planning; that the scheme of work for the subject was being adhered to; and that there was evidence that assessment was being planned for.

Weekly plans

The focus of weekly monitoring was to ensure that there were clear learning purposes set for lessons; that there was evidence of differentiation; and that any assessment opportunities which had been identified in the termly plan were being carried out during the identified week.

Curriculum coordinators were asked to identify six staff per term and to monitor two weekly forecasts of each, giving a total of twelve monitored weekly forecasts per term. Procedures for monitoring were also agreed. Each coordinator:

- was to keep a copy of each monitoring form in his or her file; a copy was given to each teacher and to the headteacher

- was to be responsible for taking any necessary action regarding monitoring of the curriculum: for example, making time to talk to individuals, informing Key Stage coordinators or the headteacher of generic problems

The school acknowledged that the extra work that was being asked of each coordinator was significant and monitoring of planning was completed in directed time after school but in lieu of other meetings. The equivalent of three hours per term was planned in for this activity.

The headteacher continued to monitor weekly planning with the focus on the coverage of the curriculum. In addition, the headteacher agreed with the senior management team a specific focus for additional monitoring of the weekly plans, which were then shared with staff. One term dealt with differentiation, one with how children were grouped and one with the strategies used for teaching reading.

EVALUATION

At the end of the year, each curriculum coordinator was interviewed to discover strengths and weaknesses of the system and ways forward.

Strengths

- All coordinators felt that they had a greater knowledge and understanding of their subject across the whole school in terms of who was doing what and when, resource implications and individual strengths and weaknesses.
- All coordinators had developed a greater proactive role in relation to supporting teacher planning.
- A greater professional dialogue could now take place focusing on the curriculum subject.
- Coordinators had greater empathy for colleagues from different phase groups because of information they had.

Weaknesses

- It was very time consuming.
- It created lots of paperwork.
- Some colleagues took constructive criticism personally, not professionally.
- Monitoring planning needed to be followed up with monitoring practice and/or classroom support.

The school as a whole then debated what was to happen next and the following was agreed:

- All coordinators would still monitor yearly and termly plans.
- The curriculum area(s) being implemented during the school year, as agreed in the school development plan, would be the only ones to be monitored on the weekly procedure.
- Non-contact time should be made available to each coordinator to support colleagues in their classrooms and monitor practice.
- The headteacher and senior management team should continue to monitor planning as before with staff being involved in agreeing the termly focus.

In conclusion, the most important issue raised throughout this chapter is the need for a whole-school approach to the creation of a framework for school development planning, curriculum documentation and monitoring, and the subsequent content that is built around this framework. Provided that there has been staff involvement and participation, then this uniformity of approach should lead a school to be able clearly to state:

- what its plans, priorities and targets are
- what is being delivered as a result of the school development plan
- how the curriculum is being delivered
- how the school monitors and evaluates teaching and learning performance
- what review mechanisms and monitoring procedures are in place and working effectively

Given that the above exists then quality should be assured. The school becomes a self-reviewing organisation improving the performance of all people involved in its life, together with the quality of the goods they provide. Planning is the vital ingredient: failing to plan is tantamount to planning to fail.

Figure 3.1 Key planning processes

Select the purpose and criteria for success

- *Audit* all aspects of the school
- *Define*, re-define school aims
- *Examine* trends and forecasts
- *Identify* priorities
- *Generate* different ways of achieving the purpose

Write the development plan

Put the chosen plan into action

- *Implement*
- *Review* continually
- *Monitor* and evaluate

Figure 3.2 Curriculum planning

Audit/review/write

- Where are we now?

- Where do we want to be?

- How are we going to achieve this?

Implement

- Take action, build in continual review

Evaluate

- Did we achieve what we set out to achieve?

Figure 3.3 Geography policy statement

Entitlement

Every child's entitlement to geography is achieved through the teaching of the School's Geography Scheme which is in line with National Curriculum requirements. Teachers exercise their professional judgment as to how the time allocation of fifty-five minutes a week is distributed throughout the term and year.

Curriculum aim

Geography is taught to extend the children's knowledge and understanding of their own environment and the world beyond. The purpose of geography teaching is to develop skills for life, empathy with others and the understanding of cause and effect.

Cross-curricular links

Geography enables access to skills of investigation, oracy, numeracy, communication and can be linked to all curriculum areas through the development of the above skills.

The National Curriculum

Geography accords with the statutory requirements of the National Curriculum and the school's scheme reflects this in the use of learning purposes, key questions, skills and content in each of the geographical themes taught.

Approaches to teaching and learning

Teachers should use a variety of approaches to deliver geography, including the following:

- whole-class lessons
- paired investigations
- fieldwork
- group based work
- individual activities

IT should be used where appropriate, and should include elements of word processing, data base work and the use of simulations.

The assessment, recording and reporting of geography must conform with the school's policy.

Figure 3.4 Guidelines for geography

The responsibilities of the subject coordinator are as follows:

Planning

- Coordinating the writing of policy, scheme, guidelines
- Ensuring delivery of attainment targets
- Ensuring progression across Key Stages and the whole school
- Supporting teachers' termly/weekly planning
- Monitoring delivery
- Developing resources.

Consultancy

- Providing specialist knowledge
- Developing contacts: liaising, networks
- Updating/being available for staff.

Overview

- Whole-school curriculum tracking
- School development plan links
- Evaluating learning process
- Ensuring policy into practice
- Assessment, record keeping
- Developing evidence and anthologies.

Specialist teachers

Geography is taught by the class teacher. However, it is
important to be aware of and use the skills and knowledge of colleagues
and the advisory service.

Planning

Work is planned in year groups following the scheme of work, in
accordance with National Curriculum statutory requirements. Staff
complete yearly/termly/weekly forecasts.

Yearly forecasts

Brief outline, statements, key words for topic/work covered.

Termly forecasts

Brief outline of content, with planned assessment opportunities/
reference to the National Curriculum.

Weekly forecasts

Learning purpose, content of lesson, resources, assessment and
differentiation.

Figure 3.4 Guidelines for geography (cont.)

Time allocation

In accordance with statutory requirements for KS2 geography at thirty-six hours per year.

Delivery

Teachers will use their professional judgment to deliver the curriculum depending upon the nature of the task/lesson, pupil needs, resources. Approaches include class, group, paired and individual work. Children will develop and use skills including observation, communication and recording.

Ancillary assistance

Support staff and parents are briefed on the learning purpose, content of the lesson and their role in order to maximise enhancement of the learning experience.

Resources

- *Location*: Geography books and atlases are located in the Resources Room. All mapping resources are labelled, catalogued and located in the geography drawers, as are OS maps, templates. Floor puzzles, geography jigsaws are also located here. Each year group in KS2 has its own globe.
- *Procedure*: A geography resources loan book is to be filled in when-ever resources are borrowed and returned.
- *Audit*: Geography resources will be audited by the coordinator to evaluate current resources, usage and future needs.

Fieldwork/visits

Fieldwork as identified in the school scheme to be coordinated and planned by the staff involved, in line with health and safety guidelines. Additional fieldwork opportunities are at the discretion of staff, but should have a clear learning purpose and be planned well in advance. It is important that when we visit these places we visit them as geographers.

Cross-curricular issues

The cross-curricular themes of health education, citizenship, economic and industrial understanding, careers and environmental education, alongside the multi-cultural and equal opportunities dimensions are referred to in the scheme.

Figure 3.5A First model of curriculum planning

Advantages

- More than one curriculum area can be dealt with in any one year therefore speeding up the process
- Coordinator has specialist knowledge which can be enhanced through INSET if necessary
- Coordinator will have detailed and first-hand knowledge of the documentation which will aid future monitoring.

Disadvantages

- Dangers of lack of ownership and therefore putting policy into practice
- Much INSET time will be needed to ensure dissemination.
- Coordinator may not have experience of teaching all phases and may lack knowledge to inform decisions
- In small schools some coordinators have responsibility for up to three subjects and cannot be expected to have specialist knowledge and/or time to compile documentation.

Figure 3.5B Second model of curriculum planning

Advantages

- Cross-phase representation will lead to quality of information based on experience
- Ownership and easier dissemination
- Aids whole-school understanding
- More involvement of staff will lead to policy becoming practice

Disadvantages

- The process takes longer.

Figure 3.6 Reviewing format and content

Stage 1: audit and review

- What do we do now as a school in relation to planning?
- Is this helpful to the individual teacher?
- Is it time consuming?
- Does our present planning suit our purpose?
- What is the purpose of planning?
- Do we have one set of plans for the headteacher and separate plans for ourselves which are more useful for our own needs?
- If as a curriculum coordinator you had to read another teacher's plans, could you do so easily, understanding the format and content?

Stage 2: redraft/devise new format

- Why do we need to plan?
- Who do we plan for?
- What should be in a plan?
- Would a standardised format/content make life easier: for the teacher; for any other reader?
- What should this format look like?
- What should be included as essential?

Stage 3: implement

- Should everyone or a selection of staff trial the format across all phases?
- How long are we going to trial the format?
- What if the format and content does not work for us?

Stage 4: review

- Has it worked?
- What do we need to change?
- What is not included that should be?
- Does it meet our purpose for planning?

© 1997 Anna Smith

Chapter 4

How do we monitor?

Christine Rhoden

Christine Rhoden qualified as a teacher at Margaret McMillan College in 1973. She has taught in the early years of primary schools for most of her career and since 1994 has held a senior management position, currently as quality curriculum manager at Kates Hill Primary School, Dudley. Her role has given her experience of whole-school curriculum planning and monitoring. The school's registration as the first primary school to achieve the British Standard Institute 5750 quality assurance registration has involved her in the systematic monitoring of the school's curriculum procedures which has given rise to this chapter.

Over the past few years there have been many externally imposed educational reforms: local management of schools, teacher appraisal, school development plans, National Curriculum, standard assessment tasks, assessment reporting and recording. There are radical changes arising from the Dearing Review published in 1993 and implemented from 1994. The OFSTED inspectorate gives schools a framework in which to examine the effectiveness of their organisation.

It has become clear during this period of change that, for schools to be successful, all documentation and new initiatives must be controlled and managed. This chapter sets out to show how one school has attempted to control, manage and monitor the curriculum. It will demonstrate how successful management and monitoring can affect the quality of teaching, the quality of learning and the standards achieved. There will be examples of planning strategies and documentation that have contributed to whole-school planning. Systems and structures enabling subject coordinators and senior managers to review and evaluate the effectiveness and useful-ness of these plans will be described, as will ways in which findings and action plans can be used to promote development and change.

> Given an effective school, children make better progress. Greater progress leads to greater capability and if handled sensitively, to greater confidence. In this way children's ability grows.
>
> (Mortimore *et al.* 1988: 286)

OFSTED (1994) reports that inspections have shown that school improvement, and more importantly, planning for it, has not been a strength in the majority of schools. Those that made provision for improvement and ultimately became more efficient and effective, have used a variety of strategies including monitoring and evaluation. These schools asked themselves the four questions suggested by Hargreaves *et al.* (1989):

- Where is the school now?
- What changes do we need to make?
- How shall we manage these changes?
- How shall we know if our management of change has been successful?

These questions can only be answered if we take stock, audit our present situation, and make strategic plans for improvement and development. Good curriculum planning and preparation are the keys to good teaching and learning. Improved outcomes are more likely if there are agreed ways of performing which are consistent throughout the school and have the support and commitment of all the staff. An establishment cannot be run effectively and efficiently if the areas in which staff are operating are not understood and evaluated systematically.

Prerequisites to successful monitoring need to be in place and there is a need for clear and relevant documentation. Quality documentation ensures that the aims of the school are shared. Documentation outlines clear roles and responsibilities and should be in the hands of staff responsible for its implementation. Monitoring cannot be purposeful and successful without a commitment from all staff to delivering the relevant and up-to-date documentation, schemes, policies and guidelines. Once these issues are addressed, steps can be taken to develop a systematic monitoring process.

MANAGEMENT STRUCTURE

There is a need for a management structure that allows time and resources for monitoring to take place. A well defined school development plan can ensure that provision is made for this activity to take place. Within a management structure names and titles may be different, but the roles and responsibilities within the school have to be covered.

Coleman and La Rocque (1990: 95) wrote that: 'careful monitoring of school performance [is] central to accountability, and a distinguishing characteristic of unusually effective [USA] school districts' and continuing by arguing that for monitoring to become an accepted practice there must be a commitment from all those involved.

Figure 4.1 on page 72 shows how one school devised and restructured its management system, forming a network of teams mutually supportive of each other.

A MONITORING NETWORK

Teaching teams form the first layer in the management of the school monitoring structure. The school operates a team teaching approach. There are two classes in each year group, with a class teacher for each. Working alongside these are language development teachers and, in early years, a nursery nurse. Senior managers support in year groups across the key stages.

Subject coordinators are next in the line of curriculum management. In this school, as in most, each area of the National Curriculum has a coordinator although there are no points above main scale for these responsibilities. Consequently, each teacher is a subject coordinator, fulfilling the functions detailed in the job description.

Core and foundation coordinators are next in this management system. Unlike subject coordinators these responsibilities merit a point above main scale. Their role is that of managers of the subject coordinators.

The quality team is made up of the core and foundation coordinators, the curriculum manager, the special educational needs manager and the assessment coordinator. This curriculum team, like the core and foundation team, meets regularly to discuss the outcomes of any monitoring that is taking place in the curriculum. The meetings allow the content and progression of the curriculum to be discussed, and an analysis of trends made.

The curriculum manager reports all findings discussed at the quality team meeting to the senior managers and to the headteacher.

The headteacher in this system is made aware of all that is taking place in the curriculum. The framework is such that the headteacher is enabled to sample areas of the school's curriculum provision, monitoring and evaluating chosen areas and issues.

This management framework supports the contention of Hargreaves and Hopkins (1991: 88) that:

> teachers share in the management of the school; leadership is a quality exercised by all staff, depending on the circumstances. The Head strives to be a supportive enabler, without abdicating responsibility.

The framework ensures that whole-school planning takes place and that there is an agreed system whereby the planning, monitoring and evaluation of the curriculum is a key area in the development process of the school. It also ensures that the expertise and the management qualities of the staff are used in the ongoing development of the establishment. To be effective, schools must demonstrate that this is true. There needs to be a whole-school commitment to the implementation, development and review of the curriculum. This school ensures, within the management structure, that clearly defined roles and responsibilities are shared. It also has clear lines of communication and consultation in which all staff can participate. Each member of staff has a necessary and vital role to play, not only in the maintenance of the systems, but in the development of the whole school.

Staff are encouraged to be reflective about their own performance, the achievement of the pupils and the effectiveness and appropriateness of the curriculum. The management structure helps reflection and monitoring to take place constantly and consistently.

A DESCRIPTION OF A SCHOOL'S MONITORING PROCESS

The following examples show how the monitoring process is shared with all the staff to enable its implementation to be successful. Curriculum monitoring is conducted by a network of school development teams. The quality team is responsible for monitoring and developing classroom management in relation to the school development plan priorities, with each member of the team having responsibility for an assigned year group, monitoring approaches to the development of the curriculum. The curriculum manager is responsible for ensuring that the statutory requirements are met and that there is continual development and improvement, continuity and progression and quality learning and teaching. The core subjects coordinator is responsible for ensuring progression and continuity in planning and delivery and for monitoring the standards of achievement in the core subjects and supporting staff as managers of these areas. The foundation subjects coordinator is responsible for ensuring continuity and progression in planning and delivery and for monitoring the standards of achievement in the foundation subjects and supporting staff as managers in these areas. The curriculum coordinator monitors and develops curriculum areas. Regular feedback meetings ensure the early identification of issues for action.

How the school monitors

The curriculum manager begins the first layer of forecast monitoring. For many years in staffrooms, questions have been asked about the purpose of weekly planning:

- What use is made of the plans?
- Who collects them in?
- How often are they collected?
- What are they collected for?
- Is there any feedback?

Teachers need to know if the plans have any real purpose in the management of the curriculum, and whether 'handing them in' ensures that this purpose is met. There must therefore be whole-school criteria against which the content of these plans can be matched.

Tally record

The weekly plans are collected in by the curriculum manager. Each one is checked against a tally record which includes all the statutory subjects and the priority areas designated by school policy. The tally record indicates compliance or non-compliance with:

- attainment targets and programmes of study
- agreed teaching styles
- the planning for all subjects of the National Curriculum
- plans for Religious Education
- cross-curricular links
- provision for differentiation
- details of homework
- time planned for uninterrupted sustained silent reading

Most of the content is recognisable as statutory requirements. A similar tally record can be devised to monitor the content of the planning that is made for the nursery and under fives curriculum.

These tally records do not in themselves ensure that planning is put into practice. They are more of an *aide mémoire*, a prompt to both the staff and the curriculum manager of what the content should be in each of the weekly forecasts. The tally can provide at a glance a general picture of curriculum planning, and any gaps which show can quickly be investigated by the curriculum manager or the persons concerned. Time and resources are made available for this process to happen, and all actions and outcomes are reported and recorded.

Role of the coordinator

All the weekly plans and tally sheets should be made available to the subject coordinators. In some schools there may be some staff who are reluctant to have their plans seen by others, possibly junior members of staff; but this attitude is not conducive to effective monitoring and needs tactfully to be remedied. For this to happen, the ethos or culture of the school needs to be one that embraces the capabilities of all staff in relation to the development of the curriculum. Creating the right ethos in which monitoring can take place was discussed in chapter 2, but this takes time, commitment and a specific style of management that cannot be developed overnight.

To reinforce the use and application of the tally record, there is in this school a forecasting procedure (figure 4.2 on page 73) known and agreed by all staff. To ensure that the forecasting procedure is followed the curriculum manager:

- reads, dates and signs the weekly forecasts to ensure that the priorities listed on the tally record are being met throughout the school
- records compliance and non-compliance on the tally record
- ensures that photocopies are made available and filed to allow access to other coordinators. The photocopies are filed in the curriculum manager's office

Alongside this procedure for the curriculum manager there is also a procedure for the subject coordinators to ensure that they fulfil their responsibilities.

Curriculum coordinators' forecast monitoring procedure

The core subjects coordinator, foundation subjects coordinator, assessment coordinator and other curriculum coordinators are responsible for monitoring the curriculum. They monitor the forecasts to ensure that the requirements of the National Curriculum and school policy are met throughout the school in relation to their specific areas.

The curriculum coordinators read the termly and weekly forecasts in order to monitor their own subject area. Monitoring is required at least twice a term for weekly forecasts and once a term for yearly and termly plans. Concerns are recorded on a monitoring record and the curriculum manager reads and checks these. The coordinators date and sign the forecast monitoring record when they have monitored the plans.

This may seem an unrealistic and unnecessary list of duties for coordinators to carry out, but these activities must take place if they are properly to manage their curriculum areas. Coordinators' roles have increased in importance and developed over the years, and staff need to be aware of their responsibilities. The role of the coordinator includes being a planner, a consultant, an adviser, a subject expert and having oversight of a specific area of responsibility.

In order to achieve the requirements and expectations of this role, coordinators require certain management competencies, for policy, for learning, for people and for resources, and to this end, time, resources and development training must be made available. The purpose of these management competencies is to create, maintain, review and develop the conditions which enable both staff and pupils to achieve effective learning outcomes. Through its evaluation process a school must ask the question: 'Have the coordinators in each subject area the skills and resources to execute their duties and responsibilities?' If any have not, then school development planning must try to redress the balance with the provision of suitable and appropriate training, support and advice.

The coordinators must be valued and seen to be sharing in the development and improvement of the school. If this can be achieved, then, over a period of time, there will be a positive influence on the teaching and learning taking place within the school.

Coordinators have never before carried such a burden of responsibility and accountability. It must be the duty of all school management models to support and encourage the development of coordinators wherever possible, so that answers to specific questions are known. Figures 4.3A on page 74 and 4.3B on page 75 list key questions, useful in INSET work or for self-assessment. Their role is central to the success of the curriculum, and, set within the constraints of class teaching, budgets and school development, must be carefully planned.

If coordinators are to be seen as agents of change, then action planning must be monitored carefully so that the desired outcomes can impact on the teaching and learning activities within the school. Effective co-ordination of the curriculum will ultimately lead to well informed and confident staff. Pupils' knowledge, skills and concepts will be evident and accessible through the systematic evaluation, monitoring and review cycles. In any school, the role of the coordinator must be thought of as fundamental to the development of the curriculum. As such, steps must be taken to devise a workable system for these roles to be effective.

COORDINATORS' MONITORING AND THE USE OF TIME

The school sets aside six hours each term taken from the 1,265 hours of directed time to support coordinators in their role. This time is used not only for training, but for planning and coordinator monitoring as well. Coordinators are asked to use this time to manage, resource and monitor their specific areas of the curriculum. To help the process and ensure that adequate and manageable planning takes place, coordinators are asked to write an action plan, with clear aims and objectives, realistic targets and set within realisable timescales.

The action plan encourages coordinators to plan realistically for the six hours they are allotted. An action plan is written each term, and the findings from the monitoring are recorded, and more importantly, the action taken from the findings is also described. In this way, there is evidence to support the monitoring that takes place. As with other areas of monitoring, a procedure is written, so no confusion arises regarding this task. The procedure sets out simply the task to be achieved:

- Curriculum coordinators devise an action plan relating to the improvement or development of their curriculum area for that term in line with the requirements of 1,265 hours.

- The action plan for the term is entered on the curriculum coordinators' records.
- The coordinators implement the action plan and monitor improvement through the weekly forecasts, reporting half-termly to the core and foundation subject coordinators.
- Concerns are first reported to the core and foundation subject co-ordinators and then to the curriculum manager.

Regular feedback meetings ensure that all information is disseminated to the relevant people. To support accountability, minutes of all meetings are recorded and stored. Relevant issues are discussed and fed back to the appropriate person or team. Efficiency is improved by ensuring that there is an agenda for all meetings before they take place.

NON-CONTACT TIME

Alongside general coordinator monitoring runs more specific subject monitoring. In this school the development plan identifies priority areas. The content and emphasis of this is directly related to the outcomes of the various curriculum meetings. Curriculum priority areas are identified and agreed and an allocation of non-contact time is awarded accordingly. Each year a total of three areas are given half a day each week for a term to monitor highlighted developments documented in the development plan. Planned curriculum monitoring may be the result of findings from coordinators' continuous monitoring of forecasts, of their scrutiny of children's books, or it may arise from the advice of external inspectors or advisers. The use of the non-contact time is documented in an action plan, detailing how the time is to be used.

One essential aim for the use of this time is to visit classrooms, so that subject coordinators have the opportunity to see at first hand the teaching and learning that is taking place in their subject area. Classroom observation plays an essential part in monitoring the curriculum, because schools must be sensitive to any anxieties of their staff a school climate must be developed which is conducive to frank and trusting two-way dialogue. In order to achieve this, the school in question arranged an INSET day where concepts and principles of monitoring were discussed. The results of the day proved invaluable, and led to a successful monitoring programme being introduced. The staff agreed on these prerequisites:

- There must be an environment which nourishes personal growth and rejects the assumption that it is a sign of weakness to admit the need for support and help.
- There must be a climate where all staff feel accepted, understood and valued.
- Staff must be concerned with personal growth, believing self-appraisal comes before self-development.

- Staff must believe that professional skills cannot be developed in isolation.
- Staff must be confident and desire feedback about their teaching ability.

It must be said that coordinators are not the only staff who need to evaluate the teaching and learning taking place. At this school, teaching teams are encouraged, at weekly planning meetings, to discuss the teaching and learning that has occurred during that week. Critical self-evaluation within a team situation is encouraged and constant development and improvement positively embraced.

Within the management structure, there are mechanisms whereby the headteacher and senior staff can be advised of areas that require change or development. It is not suggested that a system like this can be developed quickly, but if carefully planned, a process can be systematically set in place. Whole-school development is an ongoing, long-term activity and must progress at a realistic pace to ensure its future success.

SENIOR STAFF AND MANAGERS

In supporting the staff in their specific monitoring roles, there is a need for senior managers also to be proactive in curriculum monitoring. Senior staff usually have the most experience and expertise within a school organisation. As such, their involvement in curriculum and school development should be a positive one. It is not sufficient for these key members of staff to be merely carrying out roles of school 'maintenance', important as this is; they should also be actively involved in the progression and development of all aspects of the teaching and learning that is taking place in their schools.

Within this school's monitoring structure, senior staff play their part. The curriculum manager devises a monitoring timetable for senior staff in line with all other monitoring that is taking place. This monitoring is less subject based, and concentrates on the generic areas of school work. The deputy monitors teaching and learning strategies. This will take into account the school's policy on teaching and learning. The curriculum manager monitors for continuity and progression, monitoring for a coherent curriculum across the whole school. The special needs manager specifically monitors for differentiation and the able child. The headteacher monitors any area of curriculum focus based on information fed back from curriculum teams at senior management meetings.

In line with the monitoring policy of the school, senior staff use agreed criteria and will inform staff when a monitoring visit will take place. Written reports will be made in line with policy that has been agreed by all staff members. These reports detail the monitoring outcomes and, most importantly, have a space for staff to respond.

WHAT ARE THE OUTCOMES OF THIS MONITORING?

Issues will be discussed with individual staff. An action plan will be drawn up between the observer and the observed. A review date will be agreed, together with targets where appropriate, when the results of the new action plan will be evaluated. Strengths and weaknesses will be discussed. After the monitoring forms have been seen by staff, they are stored in the headteacher's office. A regular review of this general monitoring takes place at senior management meetings. It is from the recorded minutes of these and other review meetings that future INSET and, ultimately, the school development plan will be influenced. Curriculum development will be the direct result of evidence gathered during curriculum monitoring.

Results may identify individual development needs, areas of the curriculum where external advice and support is needed, or it may reveal a whole-school issue that needs to be addressed. There is need of evidence to support development and improvement and this can best be collected by 'hands-on' experience of the areas in which improvement is desired.

CONCLUSION

It has been shown that monitoring can be part of a whole-school development plan. Well managed, it can be accepted and purposeful. However, monitoring must be seen by all the staff in a school as a tool for development, for the pupils and themselves, and not just another measure to support accountability.

Peters (1987: 482) writes that 'measuring what's important should be a guiding premise for any organisation's development'. We can all 'measure', but it is what we do with the measurements that is important. It would be totally unmanageable and impracticable to monitor all things all of the time. The phrase 'a busy fool' comes to mind: everyone running around monitoring this and monitoring that, but achieving nothing. A systematic and realistic programme must be agreed and implemented if the school is to have any chance of progressing and developing.

The school that has formed the basis of this chapter has demonstrated a commitment to achieving a trained and confident staff that have the competencies to fulfil their responsibilities. They have in place a set of working procedures to ensure all personnel know and understand their roles and responsibilities.

The management structure encourages and demands continual review and reflection at all levels, and by so doing, supports the school in its continual development and improvement. With commitment and careful planning all schools can achieve a structured monitoring programme. It will not be 'quick' and it will not be easy. It is essential to handle the whole process sensitively, ensuring whole-staff participation at all stages. A school policy for monitoring should be in place with staff taking ownership of all its principles, processes and practices. Staff have to be aware of the need for improvement and see the monitoring policy as a method for moving the school and individuals forward.

As schools, we must endeavour to move away from the central government's idea that performance can only be measured by SAT results, exam results and league tables. These, of course, are important, but there is more to the quality of education offered – we need to have evidence of the excellent teaching and learning that takes place.

Rumbold (1989) wrote in the *Times Educational Supplement*: 'It is our job to make sure that parents recognise that there are other things going on in schools to prepare pupils for the world of work and life after school.' Monitoring is one sure way of achieving this – collecting evidence and working positively with the findings. Schools must, in their aims and objectives, decide what it is they are trying to achieve – but more importantly, decide and plan how they will monitor it. If these issues are addressed, a school can take stock, review, audit, act and move forward, and monitoring at all levels will be an intrinsic part of the education process in our schools.

APPENDIX

A set of the documents and proformas used in the school, many of which are mentioned in the chapter, can be obtained by sending a foolscap envelope to:

The Quality Manager
Kates Hill Primary School
Peel Street
Dudley
West Midlands

Please enclose a cheque for £5 to cover duplicating and postage.

Contents

- Management network for smaller schools
- Year planner grid
- Termly forecast grid
- Tally record
- Tally record for under-fives curriculum
- Forecast monitoring record
- Curriculum coordinators' record
- Monitoring report form
- Example of curriculum coordinators' forecast monitoring
- Evaluation criteria for classroom management
- Tally record for classroom delivery and management
- Format for action slips
- Monitoring form for continuity and progression
- Monitoring form for differentiation
- Curriculum audit checklists

Figure 4.1 A monitoring network

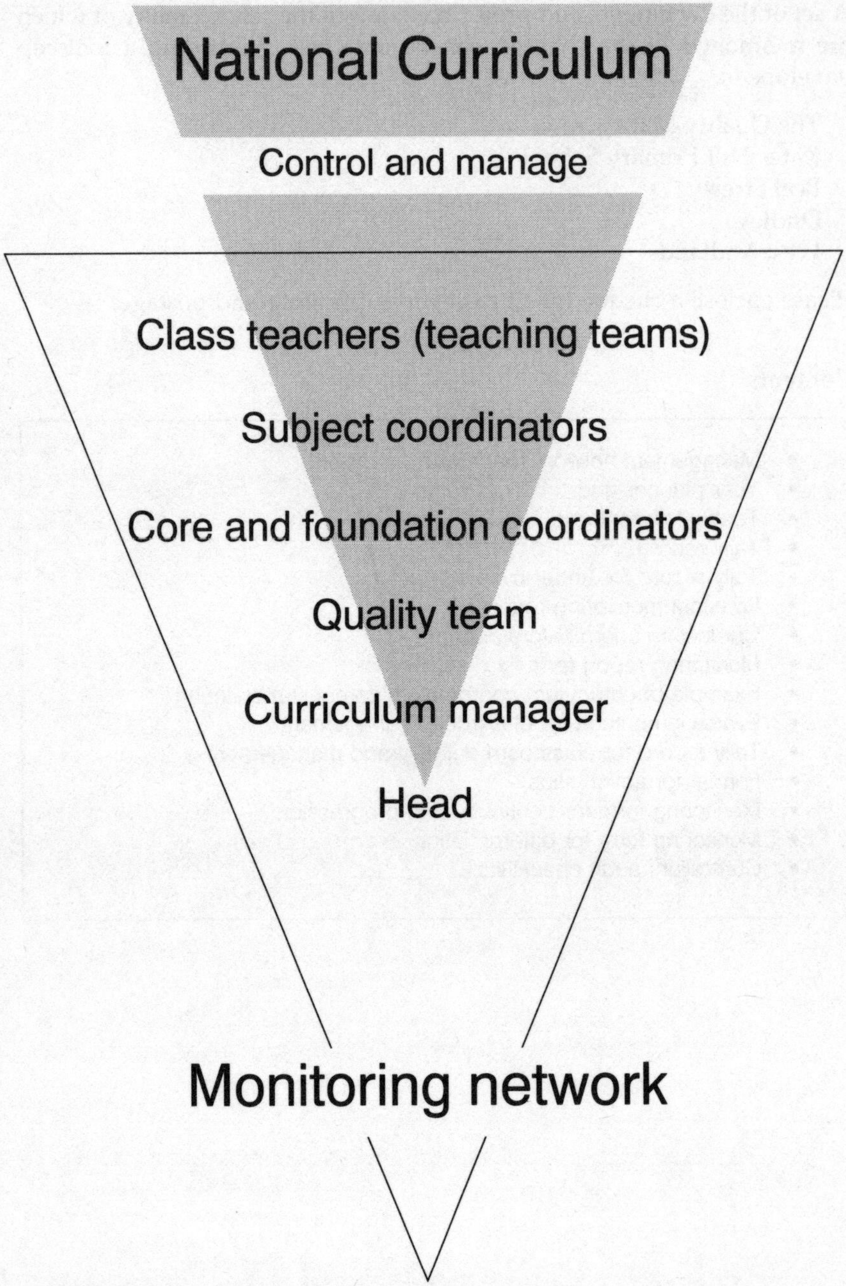

National Curriculum

Control and manage

Class teachers (teaching teams)

Subject coordinators

Core and foundation coordinators

Quality team

Curriculum manager

Head

Monitoring network

Figure 4.2 Forecasting procedures

Objectives

This procedure is to ensure that:

• Forecasting is carried out uniformly throughout the school.
• There is continuity and progression of learning.
• The requirements of the National Curriculum are met.

Responsibilities

• The responsibility for forecasting lies with the teaching teams.
• The responsibility for ensuring that this procedure is carried out lies with the quality manager.

Forecasting procedure

• Teaching teams plan for the year and the term. Termly forecasts are submitted to the quality manager for signing during the first two weeks of a new term.
• Teaching teams plan weekly forecasts and submit them to the quality manager.
• Teachers sign the assessment evidence column when the week's planning has been completed and the evaluation column when the lesson has been taught.
• All forecasts are monitored and records kept.

• *Responsibility* for the monitoring and control of the curriculum lies with the quality manager, the quality team, the staff development coordinator and the curriculum coordinators.
• *The quality manager* reads, dates and signs the termly forecast to ensure that the term's work has been planned in accordance with National Curriculum and records compliance and non-compliance on the appropriate form.
• *Curriculum coordinators* are responsible for monitoring the termly and weekly forecasts to ensure that the requirements for their subject areas are met.

Figure 4.3A Questions for coordinators

- Is there a curriculum policy?
- Are there schemes of work?
- Have guidelines been produced?
- How is the policy monitored?
- What priority has it in the development plan?
- How is coverage of all attainment targets achieved?
- How is it assessed?
- Is there a portfolio of evidence associated with this subject?
- If so, how is it updated?
- How is work marked?
- How are records kept?
- What are the time allocations throughout the school?
- How is planning done?
- How are continuity and progression ensured?
- What are your responsibilities as coordinator of this subject?
- Do you get any time for this?
- How is the work delivered in school?
- Is there a published scheme in use?
- Is the area well resourced and how are resources purchased?
- Is use made of specialists?
- Is use made of adults other than teachers?
- Are groups withdrawn?
- How do you plan for differentiation?
- What about special educational needs?
- How are staff kept informed?
- How are staff trained?

Figure 4.3B Further questions for coordinators

- What is involved in your role as coordinator?
- Do you have a job description?
- What aspect of your job description are you currently working on?
- How are you actually carrying out that element of your role?

- Do you have any non-contact time for your role?
- How do you use that time?
- Do you have an opportunity to discuss your role with your headteacher on a regular basis?

- When was the policy/scheme last reviewed? When is it to be reviewed again?
- How is such a review carried out?
- How do you know what children are learning in your subject area?
- What opportunities exist for discussion of your role and area with other teachers within the school? From other schools?
- How do you keep up to date with developments in your curriculum area?
- Do governors/parents know about developments taking place in your curriculum area?

Chapter 5

Monitoring in the classroom

Adrian Slack

Adrian Slack has worked in Dudley for eleven years, first as advisory teacher for Information Technology and since 1989 as deputy head of his present school. His interest in monitoring began as a result of attending courses on quality systems and the evaluation of school effectiveness. In 1994 he began implementing whole-school monitoring procedures and has since run courses in monitoring for his own and other LEAs. He was instrumental in his school's achievement of the Investors in People award in 1995.

The most difficult aspect of monitoring is understanding that we are looking at the delivery of the curriculum and not at the individual. This is where classroom monitoring differs from classroom observation in appraisal. With appraisal we are looking at the individual teacher with a view to promoting improvement as part of the staff development programme. Classroom monitoring must not involve personalities but keep to the delivery of the curriculum. The success of this approach will very much depend on interpersonal skills and experience.

There are many facets of the busy classroom that come under the scrutiny of the monitor. It is important that the specific criteria are shared before entering the classroom and that the criteria are adhered to. It would be unreasonable to expect that all aspects of the school's policies were observable at one time in one classroom. It will often be the case that a member of staff will avoid a difficult area of the presentation in order to make sure that whatever is being monitored is seen at its best. This is human nature and does not detract from the premise of the monitoring system.

Education students were accustomed to having their practice monitored. They knew that it was essential in order to judge whether or not they were fit for the job. This, although it caused stress for some, was accepted by all who entered a teacher training course at a college of education or a post-graduate course at university. Good paper-work, good grades in assignments did not necessarily mean that a person could teach.

With the new school-based courses there has been a move away from this style of teacher training and external observations are less frequent. For teachers to have their classroom performance monitored or to be required to monitor the performance of others is a new experience for most: either they have not experienced it in their training; or, despite the introduction of appraisal at the beginning of the decade, they have not been regularly appraised; or, as experienced teachers, they feel strongly that it is inappropriate to be checked on and, as far as they are concerned, they have nothing to learn or to justify.

This then is the less than positive climate within which we have to set classroom monitoring. Appraisal, properly and regularly conducted, has done much to minimise teacher concerns and is a welcome vehicle to promote successful observation in the classroom. Appraisal should now be embedded in the systems in every school and implicit in appraisal are two classroom observations. The difficulty is that appraisal only occurs for each member of staff on a two-year rolling programme whereas classroom observation, if it is to be effective, must occur on a regular and frequent cycle all through the self-monitoring school. Although schools have gained something from breaking down negative attitudes towards classroom observation, they have still much to do in order to embed it in the system. Schools need, therefore, to create a climate specifically for classroom observation, mainly for the purposes of monitoring the curriculum, and they need to set it in a context that is accepted and understood by all staff.

THE CONTEXT

First of all there is no merit in any teacher or senior manager doing any classroom monitoring if there are not whole-school systems in place. There needs to be an awareness of policy, aims for teaching and learning throughout the school, and a common understanding of their application to each curriculum area. There also needs to be sound mid-term and short-term planning in place. Without this there can be no criteria whereby to judge the success of classroom monitoring. Indeed, it might well be counter-productive to start classroom monitoring without this solid framework in place. Yet, without this framework, outside agencies, the LEA or OFSTED, will offer feedback on classroom monitoring using only their own criteria and not heed those established collectively within the school. A school which feels that it is not yet ready for the establishment of its own process of classroom monitoring, or is not yet confident of what it has set up, might enlist the help of its LEA in order to have some feedback. It is also useful to have the LEA evaluation of the process even when a school has a vigorous programme of classroom monitoring because it adds credibility when it can be seen that the staff of the school are in unison. Schools need to have an affirmation from the LEA that this is indeed the picture arising from their monitoring.

CREDIBILITY OF MONITORING

It is important that the school sets up a system that is judged credible by all those who are operating it. It must be supported by the teachers who are being monitored and also by those who will be required to monitor the practice in colleagues' classrooms. These may be senior managers or curriculum coordinators or indeed the headteacher. It is important that there is also a good system of classroom support in the school. Teachers will always feel the value of this because they rarely have the global view of the school that a senior manager has. This system of support needs to be balanced with the monitoring. It would be folly for a senior manager to turn up in a classroom to monitor when previously there had been no contact with or support for that class. Teachers need to see that there is a reciprocal role in monitoring. Often an outcome of monitoring is that it becomes evident that more support is needed in a particular area.

Headteachers who visit classrooms only when they are monitoring will simply create a stress situation and consequently have little positive effect on the delivery of the curriculum. In some schools there is a movement of staff in and out of classrooms and teachers become immune to any concern about being observed. In others, staff are still very insular in their classes and would like to be able to lock the door on all comers. For these teachers there will be obvious difficulties over the acceptance of class-room monitoring. It is important that the school management is aware of this and gradually brings about a change of attitudes.

There is more emphasis now on parental help in the classroom. This can be beneficial in encouraging teachers to break down the insularity of their classrooms. Nevertheless it must be remembered that parents are not trained professionals and that their observation may be misdirected. It helps, therefore, if the aims of the self-monitoring school are explained in general terms to all parents, and to those who help in classrooms, more particularly.

SETTING THE CLIMATE

Once we know that all paperwork systems are in place and that we have credibility for our system of support throughout the school, then we need to be able to set the climate for getting into the classroom. This needs to be done with the whole staff and in such a way that they not only take on what would seem to be this troublesome burden of monitoring class-room delivery, but positively welcome it as being supportive in their desire to achieve the best for the children.

Setting the climate can best be achieved by spending as much time with staff, individually and collectively, as is necessary to explain what monitoring is about and why the school needs to engage in it. Any fears must be put to rest before a programme of classroom monitoring is embarked upon. It is important always to bear in mind that staff will have more ownership of the process if reasons relate to their school and not to some national criteria or government body. The key to a school's successful introduction of self-monitoring is 'We want to do it because it is better for us and for the pupils'.

WHY MONITOR CLASSROOM PRACTICE?

How do we achieve staff support? Figure 5.1 on page 87 will be useful to the school INSET coordinator in any training session on school self-monitoring. The points it makes are intended to be debated with staff and the climate must be such that staff members feel free openly to question the validity or the practicality of any of the statements. There are many constraints on the teaching profession now that could quite easily get in the way of our purpose. The role of the teacher is becoming both more diverse and more demanding. Yet, whatever the demands, it is important that teachers can step back and look at their achievements in order to attain the highest possible quality results for their school.

The analogy in figure 5.1 that compares education to baked beans may not sit easily with teachers who feel that there is no common ground between products such as these and the education of a child. However, when teachers learn to accept that on an assembly line a tin of beans has many processes to go through, each of which is monitored through quality control procedures, then the comparison has some validity. A factory cannot afford to assume, until the customers complain, that all is well on the production line. No more can a school. If we do not monitor classroom practice then someone else will. The information that is then fed back is not developmental but may be highly critical and damaging to the school's reputation.

When we are assessing children's work in class and at home we should be looking for what is good and celebrate it. The same philosophy holds true for monitoring. Headteachers must be told by those who monitor about the effectiveness and shortcomings of classroom practice in their schools. It is important therefore that there is a system in place whereby they can routinely be informed, and that this is regarded by all staff as a natural and valuable process, both for them and for the school. There is no other way to confirm that 'what we say is what we do' other than by gaining the evidence from watching classroom delivery.

Teachers must have as their main purpose the welfare and progress of the children. If they do not, then the profession has lost its way through an excessive concern for organisation and administration instead of a proper concern for teaching. Classroom monitoring will inform teachers on the extent to which the school's organisation is geared primarily to the improvement of the children's learning.

It is sometimes valuable, certainly in a training session, to stand the discussion on its head and ask staff members if they can provide arguments for not being held to account through monitoring. They may argue that, if they feel confident that they are doing a good job, is there any point in confirming it by having someone watch them?

The value of monitoring is not purely critical. As with children's work, it is important for teachers also to celebrate that which is good. With classes that keep themselves very much to themselves monitoring might very well enable some good practice to become evident which can be shared with other classes around the school. Many schools are, whether they like it or not, caught up in a competitive education system. If they do not take every opportunity for collaborative improvement then they may well lose out, financially and in public regard.

Finally, it is important that schools know where their weaknesses are so that they can turn them into strengths. It is better to be part of a system where teachers can discover weaknesses for themselves and not wait for somebody else to tell them.

HOW TO MONITOR CLASSROOM PRACTICE

Figure 5.2 on page 88 is a valuable summary of how to monitor and can be used in a training session or as a personal check sheet. Children are the best source of information about their learning: they are usually well aware of how the system is impinging on them. When asked, they are likely to offer information on whether their work is too hard or too easy, whether they enjoy it and whether they get adequate feedback from the teacher on their progress. Some teachers might claim that this is a dubious, even unprofessional, source of information; yet on the whole, provided this is not the only data used, the children's perceptions can be a valuable source of information in the monitoring process.

Additionally, tracking a child, seeing him or her at work over a period of time in a full range of learning areas, gives useful information on how the curriculum is having an impact.

It is clearly essential that teachers share what constitutes good teaching and learning. There are many documents that set this out, not least the OFSTED *Framework for Inspection*. Comparing these documents needs to be part of the INSET so that all staff are aware of what is required of them before anyone enters their classroom to monitor practice. As in appraisal, there needs to be a focus for a monitoring visit, as all criteria cannot and should not be looked at simultaneously. There needs to be an understanding that the person monitoring is not someone who necessarily knows more than the class teacher but is rather someone who can stand outside the activity and contribute useful observations, derived perhaps from particular areas of expertise. In primary schools this is important since staff have to try to be experts in all subjects. It is vital that there is regular and early feedback and that the outcomes of classroom monitoring are not just passed to the senior management and filed away

Monitoring will be a two-way process in that monitors may well learn about aspects of the primary curriculum or its delivery that are new to them. For example, it is rare that senior managers in a primary school are expert practitioners in the full range from reception to year six, with an up-to-date knowledge of the content and methodology in all the subjects of the curriculum; but in monitoring they will enhance their own learning by thoughtful listening and by posing questions to the teacher after the session. This can help all parties to reflect on what is the best way forward. There have often been instances where a second opinion is needed to prompt someone to think about their practice. Non-aggressive questioning is more likely to lead to improvement than pontification.

Weaknesses should not be overlooked. This may happen if a close colleague is monitoring and falls into the 'buddy syndrome' where it is more important not to upset a friend than to improve practice. This is a very difficult issue and may require one-to-one inservice training but, where feedback is always professional and not personal, criticism is usually acceptable. With any system it is important to be able to find solutions. After the feedback, difficulties must be analysed and dealt with, if necessary at senior management level. What are the reasons for any discrepancies between the school's aims and the teacher's practice? It may be that this is nothing to do with the teacher but with the organisation of the school, or the way that a particular system has been set up, or a lack of resources. All these problems are highlighted by a good monitoring report and teachers are usually grateful that these issues have come to the attention of the senior management so that something can be done.

WHAT TO MONITOR?

Classroom monitoring can cover a vast area as there are so many facets to the primary curriculum. The task should be sub-divided and allocated to staff on a rolling three-year programme within the school development plan. It is always difficult to predict priorities over the full three years and it will be necessary to revise the programme annually to meet priorities. What is essential is that funds are allocated to release staff for monitoring. For the primary school classroom teacher, the curriculum coordinator may be the monitor. For more senior staff it is likely to be a member of the senior management team, which has the added responsibility of ensuring that there is feedback to staff, headteacher and governors.

The monitors will initially want to discover that what has been planned by the school is actually being delivered in the curriculum areas. This is the most straightforward aspect of monitoring because it only involves checking that the planned content matches the actual content. However, monitors must be sure that they know the schemes and guidelines in advance of their monitoring visit. They need additionally to look at the teachers' mid-term and short-term planning and compare this with delivery in the classroom.

Monitors should have a set number of sessions allocated, the number depending on the size of the school, the number of monitors available and, of course, the budget. The criteria for observation should be shared with each member of staff prior to the lesson, as it is for appraisal. This only needs to be a brief meeting because the programme of monitoring should be known to all staff well in advance. There is no merit in surprising staff by turning up unannounced in their classroom to monitor. This will simply lead to suspicion of the monitor's motives and achieve no tangible results. The practice of regular monitoring provides enough pressure in itself to maintain the necessary rigour.

Monitoring must also be followed with support where needed. The headteacher will be aware of the monitoring programme from the school development plan and will be able to know where the pressure and support, the twin ingredients that help to accomplish results, should be at any one time.

For monitors to look at more than the delivery of the content of the curriculum might have repercussions on the role of the INSET coordinator who is responsible for all training needs. Those running courses for monitors are now putting a greater emphasis on teaching and learning within each subject area. These courses also offer guidance and support not only on the latest developments in content but also on how to deliver the subject in a way which will improve results.

When coordinators are able to monitor the teaching and learning going on in the classroom in their subject then they may find merit in using figure 5.3 on page 89. This will help a less experienced monitor to deal with some simple criteria that can be picked up easily from looking around the room and sampling the atmosphere of the class.

Each school currently has the option as to whether or when the four-year-olds should take up the National Curriculum. Under present legislation, they do not need to do this until the term after they are five; but there are many schools which prefer this to be done earlier so that the work of the class is not divided. If this is the case it is important that the children do not miss out on their early development.

Having mutually acceptable criteria is useful for the important partnership between monitor and monitored. It is, of course, impossible to attempt to look at all the criteria at once. The pre-meeting allows monitors to highlight certain aspects that they want to look at and to inform the member of staff. This meeting is not about choices as in appraisal; there is no negotiation on what will be observed. Having decided the criteria it is important that the plan is adhered to. Not to do this will cause undue pressure and will be counter-productive.

CLASSROOM OBSERVATION

Classroom observation for monitoring purposes is very different from that for appraisal or classroom support. In appraisal only a brief amount of time is spent in the classroom in order to gather data which is then used to set the appraisal interview in context. In the self-monitoring school the monitor is looking specifically at the delivery of the curriculum by that teacher and is not directly concerned with staff or curriculum development. There is a need for a shared understanding of what the monitor is looking for from the teacher, and figure 5.4 on page 90 provides a list. It is important that both the teacher being observed and the monitor do not fall into the trap of thinking it vital that every item on this list must be covered. However, this is a valuable INSET document for staff to become aware collectively of the many facets of their role as teachers and monitors.

There are problems over being at one and the same time part of the activity of the classroom and the monitor and observer of what is going on. The monitor needs to decide therefore how to keep out of the action. Once monitoring becomes common practice children will not be unduly aware of the monitor's presence.

It is vital that at some stage monitors move around the classroom and talk to the children, taking care, nevertheless, not to fall into a support role. How the monitor takes notes must be agreed with the class teacher in advance. Because note-taking is common in most appraisal observations staff will usually find this no problem. Most will prefer that the monitor takes notes rather than relies on memory. In talking to children, monitors will find that the learning criteria in figure 5.5 on page 91 are a useful basis for asking pertinent questions; but the language in which they are couched must of course be adapted to the age group.

All this information must be consolidated in a report on the observation which is shared with the teacher. This gives teachers an opportunity, as with the appraisal report, to register their dissent, but, primarily, discussion helps to make them reflect and bring about improvement.

FEEDING BACK INFORMATION

Feedback is vital to the success of the system. It is important that INSET sessions have clarified with staff how they would like the information fed back. Some may be satisfied with a verbal communication while others may wish to see the written report. Whatever staff favour, individually or collectively, there must in any case be a written record of the monitoring activity which can be studied when the senior management team is evaluating evidence of school improvement. If monitoring is not having a tangible effect on the teaching and learning then there is no point in doing it.

However much staff have been prepared for monitoring there will still be reservations about it. Some staff object to having their space invaded, as they see it. Monitors must understand such feelings and be sensitive to them. There is a need constantly to create a friendly professional atmosphere and to make clear that the role of the monitor is to look at the delivery of the curriculum and not the teacher as an individual.

It is always frustrating for a teacher if feedback is delayed, though there may at times be good reasons for this. Some immediate response to the observation is nevertheless imperative. OFSTED has a code of practice that an observer does not simply walk out of the room without any comment.

Monitoring is a two-way process and there may be circumstances that explain certain occurrences in a classroom. It is important to the monitor to hear about these as they may have some bearing on measures for improvement. Some members of staff may wish to comment on the written report, and space for that should be made available. As with children it is important to emphasise the positive and question the discrepancies so that dialogue is promoted and solutions found.

It is not good policy for monitors at feedback to emphasise the positive at the beginning and leave negative aspects until the end. When this becomes common knowledge, a 'bottom line syndrome' is created where staff are less interested in the meat of the report because they are waiting to hear what the problems are. This makes the whole report appear to be negative. It is very important that morale is boosted through these reports. Figure 5.6 on page 92 is valuable both during INSET on feedback and as an *aide mémoire*, not only to monitors but to the staff as a whole.

Monitoring reports provides a means whereby success can be celebrated. Therefore the text of the report should include both positive and negative points as they arise. Above all, the teacher must be left with a good understanding of what has been observed if the report is to be useful as a planning and improvement tool.

Any decision about who sees the report must be a matter for discussion by the whole staff. Because the report is a professional document this should not be an issue; but there will still be some teachers who have reservations about the report's availability to others. It is important to remember that this is not a confidential report as in appraisal but a means to check that what we say is what we do. If there is a hierarchical system of management with phase leaders, then it is sensible that immediate managers see the reports so that they can promote changes in practice if this is advisable.

Schools with more than one form in each year should monitor year groups concurrently and deliver a report that encompasses the whole year group. This encourages closer planning and delivery of the curriculum. One of the possible problems in a large school is that year groups do not work sufficiently collaboratively. Good classroom monitoring can help to alleviate this problem.

All points made in the reports must be such that action may be set in train in order to make improvements. If the process of monitoring and feeding back does not improve the quality of the education for the child then there is little purpose in doing it. Time for evaluation of the process must be built in to the school's INSET to ensure that there is a rolling programme of revisits so that continuous progress can be seen and measured.

MANAGEMENT ISSUES

Monitoring in the classroom is not an end in itself and the results must be followed up with an action plan and further review of the systems in place in school. It is vital if the school is to become a self-evaluating one that monitoring is made a priority in the school development plan and a budget is attached to it so that it will realistically happen. The headteacher and deputy must do more than solely release people to monitor. Inservice training will be required for many staff in order to give them the skills to be able to pick out what is good and bad in a classroom situation as well as to convey this to teachers, some of whom will be their seniors in age and experience. It is with this in mind that the early reports could well be shared first with the senior management so that a plan for feedback can be worked out.

The first phase of reporting should not attempt to cover too much ground and might with advantage concentrate on one subject throughout the school. In that way staff can be presented with a general report and deduce which parts refer to them. This, provided that it is followed up with more in-depth monitoring, works well and gives a global view to all the staff. Until they have been given some training in interpersonal skills staff may well find difficulty in reporting back findings directly to other members of staff. This part of the role of the coordinators will have to grow as they gain more experience.

In reporting back it might be discovered that there are aspects of the management structure that are flawed. This has to be borne in mind when reports are written and, if there is to be progress, then management must be as reflective as the teachers are being asked to be. A lack of resources is often highlighted as a major problem in the delivery of the curriculum. A good monitoring system will provide evidence of problems such as these.

In a school which has prepared well through INSET and where the monitoring process is itself under regular review, the improvement that will be observable both in the quality of the teaching and in the pupil outcomes can be considerable. Perhaps the greatest merit of self-monitoring is that it is not externally imposed, but has been agreed by dialogue and consolidated by experience within the individual school.

Figure 5.1 Why monitor?

Why we need to monitor

- There is a need to promote continuous development and improvement.
- The school will be checking processes against established criteria.
- The school is working towards being a self-evaluating school that does not need external agencies to judge its success or failure.
- Quality control of any product – baked beans, for example – undergoes rigorous inspection; children's progress through the school should be similarly sampled.
- For a quality service there must be evaluation, not for mistakes, but to confirm successes and discover where improvement is possible.
- Schools need confirmation that 'what they say is what they do'.
- The school is accountable to the governing body.
- Others need to know of the school's successes.
- Teachers need to know where they can improve.

© 1997 Adrian Slack

Figure 5.2 How to monitor in the classroom

We can monitor delivery and improve classroom practice by

- Checking practice against policies, schemes and guidelines
- Checking practice against yearly/termly/weekly plans
- Talking to children in lessons
- Tracking children through school
- Sharing criteria for what is good teaching/learning
- Looking at practice using school and OFSTED criteria
- Being able to step out of the activity and comment
- Giving professional evaluation and feedback
- Raising issues together
- Establishing two-way communication
- Celebrating the good but also probing for weaknesses
- Finding the reason for difficulties
- Posing questions to stimulate reflection on practice
- All having a responsibility to monitor our areas
- Phasing teacher release in order to share practice and have knowledge of other areas of responsibility

© 1997 Adrian Slack

Figure 5.3 Tally record: classroom monitoring

Class				
Date				
Furniture well organised				
Resources available				
Trays labelled clearly				
Evidence of good presentation				
Brainstorming				
Shared purpose				
Continual and final review				
Criteria for success				
A range of tasks				
Personal projects				
Work suited to ability				
Challenging work				
Extension work provided				
Targets for completion				
Opportunities for assessment				
Progress noted and recorded				
Good display				
Children valued				
Rationale for grouping				

Figure 5.4 Monitoring criteria: teaching

Class monitored _____ **Date** _____

- Is the teaching purposeful?
- Do lessons have clear aims?
- Is time used efficiently?
- Is sufficient ground covered?
- Does the teaching create and sustain interest?
- Is a range of imaginative teaching strategies used?
- Is differentiation addressed in the activities?
- Are teachers' expectations sufficiently high?
- Are pupils with special educational needs appropriately supported?
- Is there sufficient challenge?
- Are lessons managed efficiently in an orderly manner?
- Does the planning suit the purpose of the lesson?
- Are the resources suitable for all pupils?
- How efficiently are support teachers and adults used?
- Are there useful classroom routines in place?
- Are relationships supportive?
- Is there effective interaction between pupils and teachers?
- Are explanations clear?
- Is there appropriate teacher intervention?
- Is there a sensitivity to particular needs?
- Is class assessment supportive to improvement?
- Is work marked in a consistent and positive way?
- Do teachers encourage pupils to assess their own performance?

Figure 5.5 Monitoring criteria: learning

Class monitored: ———— **Date** ————

Do pupils

- Respond to the task and challenge?
- Show a willingness to concentrate on the task and challenge?
- Make good progress?
- Adjust to the demand of working in different contexts?
- Select appropriate methods and organise the resources?
- Sustain work with commitment and enjoyment?
- Evaluate their own work and are realistic about their progress?
- Know how to improve their work?
- Work cooperatively?
- Understand the purpose of the tasks undertaken?
- Learn from their mistakes?
- Have a positive attitude to their work?
- Cope with subjects they dislike or find difficult?
- Apply learning in new contexts?
- Take part in a review of the lesson?

Figure 5.6 Feeding back information from monitoring

- Be sensitive.
- Understand reservations.
- Emphasise the positive.
- Question any discrepancies.
- Be professional, not personal.
- Stick to criteria and evidence found at the time.
- Always ask for opinion on comment.
- Summarise so that it is obvious where improvement can be made.
- Pose questions to make staff reflect.
- Check that monitoring is improving the quality of teaching and learning.

Chapter 6

Planning and monitoring provision for diversity

Robin Richmond

Robin Richmond is now an educational consultant and registered inspector of schools. He was formerly a senior LEA inspector of schools for special educational needs and inservice training. Previously he held a variety of responsibilities in both primary and secondary schools and as headteacher of a local education authority service for children with second language and learning difficulties. He has long experience as a tutor-counsellor with the Open University. He has published a number of articles on special educational needs.

The school which is concerned about responding to the learning needs, interests and capacities of all its pupils, valuing all equally, will have procedures in place to monitor both the school's response to, and the progress of the diversity of pupils in the school. Those who present schools with the greatest challenge are the small number with complex or more severe learning difficulties, probably with a statement of special educational needs. There is a larger group of children with less severe learning difficulties and a still larger group of pupils who have needs to which schools find a response difficult or to which they do not respond. The self-monitoring school must be aware of the extent to which it is responding to the challenges presented by the diversity of pupils' needs in the school.

WHOLE-SCHOOL RESPONSIBILITIES

Responding to diversity is a whole-school responsibility. The National Curriculum Council claimed that in 'both ordinary and special schools good practice is most likely to be advanced when all members of staff are committed to the aims providing a broad, balanced, relevant and differentiated curriculum, and raising standards for each of the pupils they teach' (NCC 1989: 3). Responding to diversity means providing equality of opportunity in which all pupils are valued equally irrespective of ability, culture or gender and maximum opportunities are sought for all pupils. Personal and whole-school reflection is involved to achieve the elimination of attitudes which produce low expectations and poor motivation, aspirations and achievements in pupils. In the best schools the beliefs about meeting the diverse needs of all the pupils will be articulated throughout the school's policies and in the way in which the school is structured, organised and managed. Such a school will be constantly watchful through a system of monitoring and review of its practices.

Inspecting the school response to diversity is the responsibility of all members of an OFSTED inspection team. The revised *Framework for the Inspection of Schools* (OFSTED 1995a) now identifies special educational needs and equal opportunities as separate aspects in the inspection. Teams are required to include one or more inspectors charged with inspecting or coordinating the inspection of, and reporting on the progress of, pupils with special needs, in particular, the extent to which they gain access to a broad and balanced curriculum.

The governors of the self-monitoring school are required to check that the school as a whole meets the requirements of the law. The education of pupils with special educational needs has been and is protected by separate special laws or sections of laws applying to the education of all children. The most recent law, and some would claim the most directive, is Part III of the Education Act 1993 (DFE 1993a). One important requirement is to ensure access for pupils with special educational needs to the educational and social life of the school. The duties of governing bodies are to:

- do their best to secure that the necessary provision is made for any pupil who has special educational needs 161(1)(a)
- secure that, where the headteacher or the appropriate governor has been informed by the LEA that a pupil has special educational needs, those needs are made known to all who are likely to teach him or her 161(1)(b)
- secure that teachers in the school are aware of the importance of identifying and providing for those pupils who have special educational needs 161(1)(c)
- when necessary or desirable in order to coordinate provision for pupils with special educational needs to consult the local education authority (LEA), the funding agency for schools (FAS) and the governing bodies of other schools 161(3)
- ensure that such pupils join in the activities of the school together with those who do not have special educational needs, so far as that is reasonably practicable and compatible with the child receiving the necessary special educational provision, the efficient education of other children in the school and the efficient use of resources 161(4)

- draw up and report annually to parents on their policy for pupils with special educational needs 161(5)

RESPONDING TO DIVERSITY IN THE CURRICULUM

The United Kingdom has now followed the practice of many other countries and established by the Education Reform Act (1988) the principle of a National Curriculum for all children. A National Curriculum that excludes a significant proportion of the nation's children would be a contradiction. Consequently, it has become common to refer to the 'entitlement' of individual pupils to the National Curriculum. HMI (1986) identified the features of a good curriculum as 'broad, balanced, relevant and differentiated'. Unfortunately, the Education Reform Act (DES 1988a) refers only to 'a broad and balanced curriculum including the National Curriculum' omitting any reference to 'relevance' or 'differentiation'.

One of the difficulties with the National Curriculum for many pupils has been the over-prescriptive nature of much of the content and the inflexibility of the national standard assessment tasks at the ends of Key Stages 1 and 2. The content of the National Curriculum is based on what expert opinion believes average pupils of given ages ought to know, understand and be able to do. Consequently for some children the programmes of study can cause them to experience learning difficulties.

The original National Curriculum contained brief hierarchical learning targets in the form of statements of attainment. These 'smaller steps' were useful for the creation of individual programmes for individual pupils. Statements of attainment are not included in the revised National Curriculum.

The foreword to the revised National Curriculum claims that it allows greater flexibility to respond to pupils with special educational needs. Curriculum materials, presented in age-appropriate contexts, can be used from earlier or later Key Stages to enable individual pupils to progress and demonstrate achievement.

The Warnock Report pointed out that the goals of education were the same for all pupils but drew attention to the need for a diversity of paths:

> For some pupils the road they have to travel towards the goals is smooth and easy, for others it is fraught with obstacles. For some the obstacles are so daunting that even with the greatest of possible help, they will not get very far. Never the less for them too progress will be possible and their educational needs will be fulfilled as they gradually overcome one obstacle after another on the way.
>
> (DES 1978: para. 1.4)

Education as a journey is an acceptable notion but the sense of struggle and implied shortness of the journey for some learners is a criticism of the common view of the relationship between ability and learning and the inability of many teachers to value and meet effectively the diversity of educational needs. Mortimore *et al*. (1988: 264) demonstrate that children's performance changes over time: 'Given an effective school, children make greater progress. Greater progress leads to greater capability and if handled sensitively, to greater confidence. In this way children's ability grows.'

SCHOOL EFFECTIVENESS AND DIFFICULTIES IN LEARNING

Where pupils are asked to learn inappropriate things in inappropriate ways they will experience learning difficulties. Booth (1987) argues that children with special needs are those whose needs schools, for whatever reason, fail to meet. Stradling *et al*. (1991) list examples of the school failing the pupils. If pupils enter a school with limited social or language skills and the school does not respond to those needs the school is failing the pupils. Schools do matter as Mortimore *et al*. (1988: 265) demonstrate:

> They matter in two senses: they can help pupils change and develop and also because their effects are not uniform. Individual schools matter a great deal to the pupils who attend them.

Individual features of each school's practices are not so important; but what appears to be important for any school is an agreed and consistent strategy which is monitored.

One of the key recommendations of the joint report by the Audit Commission and HMI (1992a) was that the government should define in legislation who are the pupils with special educational needs. Mittler and Pumfrey (1989) claim that 'despite the circulars and regulations generated in attempts to clarify the identification of special needs and outline the provision of interventions the term special educational needs remains sufficiently vague to mean all things to all people'. Clark *et al*. (1995) point out that what is special can only be defined by what is ordinary, and the boundary between the two constantly shifts. Consequently teachers and schools can only 'construct' and 'reconstruct' their own versions of special educational need in relation to local circumstances. Clearly, the context and setting in which children's individual difficulties manifest themselves are inseparable from an educational need being perceived as a 'special' educational need. Parents are aware of the importance of the context for the progress that their children make as they move through the primary school from one teacher to another. The perception of individual educational needs as 'special' educational needs is further influenced by the possibility of additional educational resources not normally available to children with 'ordinary' educational needs.

IDENTIFYING PUPILS WITH SPECIAL EDUCATIONAL NEEDS

Nevertheless, the Education Act 1993 lays a duty on governors to 'secure that teachers in the school are aware of the importance of identifying, and providing for those pupils who have special educational needs'. Guidance on identifying and registering such pupils, for which governors are required 'to have regard' under Part III of the Education Act 1993, is contained in a Code of Practice (DFE 1994b) on the identification and assessment of special educational needs. A process is outlined by which pupils are registered at various stages according to the severity or complexity of their educational needs. No guidance is given on what kind of difficulties pupils have to experience in order for them to be placed on the register at the first of five stages. The register is a semi-formal document, from which the number of children registered at each stage can be easily determined.

It is not unusual to include a brief description of the kind of difficulties that individual pupils are experiencing. The Code of Practice uses the terms: learning difficulty; specific learning difficulty (dyslexia); emotional and behavioural difficulties; physical disability; hearing difficulty; visual difficulty; speech and language difficulty; medical conditions. However, broad descriptions of pupils' difficulties are of little use to the teacher planning work to match individual learning needs. The self-monitoring school will have clear criteria for registering pupils at each stage and particularly for placing pupils on the register at the outset. The nature of individual pupils' difficulties and the progress they make will be checked against the criteria.

The number of children on the register is important information for the self-monitoring school. OFSTED (1996b: 6) found that there is a wide variation between schools across and within LEAs in the numbers of pupils identified as having special educational needs and claimed that identification and assessment procedures are too inconsistent. There is no accurate information as yet on the proportion of primary children on register. Bibby (1995) estimates that on average 7 per cent of a school population will be at Stage 1 of the register, 4 per cent at Stage 2 and 3 per cent at Stage 3. In addition about 1 per cent of pupils in mainstream schools have a statement of special educational needs.

Some schools are monitoring the achievements of pupils when they enter the school with baseline profiling or standardised testing of reading and repeat this as pupils move through the school to obtain some objective measure of the value-added element by the school. The report of the Audit Commission/HMI (1992a) claimed that the standard methods of testing and reporting introduced under the National Curriculum have the potential to provide schools with a measure of the level of a school's performance with pupils with learning difficulties. Other strategies by the self-monitoring school might include internally devised tests, regular observation of children's individual progress in the course of their everyday work, profiling, National Curriculum records, and reading records. Pupils' records and the accompanying assessment and monitoring arrangements are essential evidence of the progress pupils are making.

An unexpectedly large number of pupils on the register might indicate inadequacies in the match of the content and process of the curriculum to pupils' needs. If staff are passing responsibility for children whom they find difficult to teach to the special needs coordinator then a review of teaching and learning strategies in the school might be called for. Commenting on practices in urban schools, OFSTED (1993a) found that children's abilities on entry to school were rarely assessed and, when they were, the information was not always used for planning future learning. Teachers, although often aware of pupils' limited reading and spelling skills, rarely adapted teaching strategies to take account of this.

GROUPING PUPILS FOR TEACHING

The allocation of pupils to different teaching groups is a strategy adopted by some schools to respond to learning needs. The withdrawal of pupils from their normal classes for short periods for individual or small group teaching is not uncommon. OFSTED (1996a) has found that in most primary schools, even within mixed ability classes, pupils are often grouped by ability for mathematics and English and that this often led to a better match of work to pupils' needs.

Alexander et al. (1992) were in favour of placing children in different ability groups for particular purposes but drew attention to research in the 1960s which showed that, while streaming in primary schools could benefit the achievement of the most able pupils, pupils in lower streams tend to see themselves as failures and develop a poor self-image. They concluded that 'streaming is a crude device which cannot do justice to the different abilities a pupil may show in different subjects and contexts' (ibid.: 22). Following a report by OFSTED (1993b), the Secretary of State for Education wrote to all primary schools asking them to consider a better match of work to children's needs, including the introduction of setting where possible, or of grouping by ability and greater use of specific subject teaching for older children in particular and greater use of specialist or semi-specialist teaching.

The self-monitoring school needs to ensure that the organisation of teaching groups is not disadvantaging or devaluing individuals and groups of pupils. For example, it may be that an excessive enthusiasm for withdrawal groups for basic skills teaching could result in a narrow curriculum denying pupils their entitlement. Pupils with behavioural difficulties might accumulate in lower ability teaching groups. Certain teachers might be perceived as 'good with less able pupils' rather than skilled teachers with any learners. With setting arrangements, assumptions might be made that the needs of the pupils in the set are identical, thus reducing the match of work to the needs of individual pupils. The self-monitoring school will be asking parents and the pupils themselves how they perceive the school arrangements for grouping pupils, and thus identifying the effect of those arrangements on their expectations, behaviour and self-image.

All classes, however constituted, contain pupils with a range of attainment, motivation and interests. Most primary pupils are taught in mixed ability teaching groups. Mixed age group classes are common and vertically grouped classes relatively rare (Alexander *et al.* 1992). In 1990 three-quarters of primary classes had fewer than thirty children and of these one in three fewer that twenty (*ibid.*: 3). OFSTED (1996b) asserted, based on the observations of independent inspectors, that at Key Stage 2 class size made no difference to the quality of pupils' learning in mixed ability primary classes. However, analysis of the inspection findings indicated that inspectors were not directed to observe or judge the effect of class size on the quality of pupils' learning. Yet teachers know the effects of increased class sizes: they have less time to interact with individual pupils and so are often forced to be reactive to pupils rather than proactive: the time available to discuss work with individuals, respond to individual needs or assess individual progress is restricted. Managing the group as a whole takes precedence over the needs of individuals.

Ironically, Her Majesty's Chief Inspector of Schools (HMCI) in his annual report (OFSTED 1996a) claimed that pupils with special needs 'were poorly served in two-thirds of the lessons they attended'. The report states that:

- Teaching failed pupils who were unable to cope with important aspects of the lesson content.
- Too frequently tasks were inaccessible to pupils with learning difficulties.
- A poor match of tasks to their abilities often had an adverse effect on the attitudes shown by the pupils in the lessons.

The self-monitoring school ought to have a policy about the principles and procedures by which class sizes are determined for particular learning purposes. Many schools operate on an assumption about class sizes, but rarely are the principles or procedures for planning class size clearly stated and therefore the effect of class size on pupils' individual needs, and particularly on special needs, cannot be monitored and subsequently reported.

PLANNING FOR INDIVIDUAL LEARNING NEEDS

Agreed approaches to, and planning for, teaching and learning are related to success in reducing the difficulties in learning experienced by pupils. As chapter 4 indicates, planning for teaching and learning includes whole-school plans and policies, Key Stage plans and policies, subject area policies and schemes of work, followed by yearly, termly and weekly plans. NFER (1995) supports this planning hierarchy for pupils with learning difficulties. The National Curriculum Council (NCC 1989) stated that curricular policies should reflect whole-school approaches to teaching and learning and be a practical guide to teaching within the school's curricular programme, and drew attention to the connection between agreed school policies on teaching and learning, success in meeting the range of individual needs and an effective response to pupils' special learning needs. All plans in school should be scrutinised for the extent to which they include the flexibility to respond to the diversity of individual needs in school. A number of questions, listed in figure 6.1 on page 113, should be asked of school policies.

Special teaching would appear to be qualitatively no different from any other teaching (Aubrey 1995). Clark *et al.* (1995) found that innovatory practice in primary schools for pupils with special needs was characterised by 'a growing reportoire of articulated strategies for teaching and learning developed within the context of the entitled curriculum'.

OFSTED (1996b: 6) found that pupils with special needs 'benefit no less than others from good teaching which takes full account of the needs of all pupils' and identified the features of good lessons for pupils with special needs in classes taught by the class teacher without additional help as:

- careful planning that takes account of the needs of all pupils
- strategic help with the teacher targeting tasks to those individuals who require more teaching help
- work that is appropriately matched to individual need and taught using a range of different pupil groupings, tasks or resources
- good procedures for assessment and recording

Good teachers watch individual pupils, assess their progress and respond to their learning needs. However, matching teaching and learning to the needs of individual pupils is not always easy. For effective teachers of pupils with learning difficulties pupil-centred teaching is a highly developed teaching skill. Aubrey (1995) suggests that pupils with learning difficulties may require not a 'special' teaching but more intensive teaching as individuals or in small groups or with the help of special support assistance, and that schools should budget to provide for this. The numbers of pupils in classes in special schools are smaller and consequently allow for more intensive teaching of individual pupils.

The report of Her Majesty's Chief Inspector of Schools (OFSTED 1996a) identified the features of good and poor teaching for pupils with learning difficulties in lessons in special schools. Features of good and poor teaching in special schools are shown in figure 6.2 on page 114.

DIFFERENTIATION IN THE CLASSROOM

Dickinson and Wright (1993) describe 'differentiation' as a planned process of intervention in the classroom. Moss (1995) emphasises different approaches to teaching. Others (Weston 1992) have discussed the wider implications of the way the term is used. Hart (1995), for example, points out that providing for 'difference' should begin with an examination of how our perceptions of 'difference' come about. Alexander *et al.* (1992: 28) were of the view that 'the idea that at any one time learning tasks in nine subjects can be exactly matched to the needs and abilities of all pupils in a class is hopelessly unrealistic'. The National Curriculum Council (1989: 1) also emphasised differentiation as taking place in lessons in that 'the majority of pupils with learning difficulties simply require work to be suitably presented and differentiated to meet their need'. Planning for differentiation involves concentrating energies on what the teacher may be able to do something about. Dean (1992) refers to some useful areas which the teacher can influence: an inability to behave appropriately in class, to understand what is required, to concentrate and learn effectively, to relate to others and the difficulties presented by lack of interest and motivation and the inappropriateness of general classwork.

A number of factors should be considered in planning for differentiation in lessons. The way pupils are to be grouped for learning, the role of the teacher in promoting learning, the nature of the learning activities, the resources required and the means by which learning is to be monitored all need consideration at the planning stage.

RESPONDING TO PUPILS WITH SPECIAL NEEDS AT STAGE 1

Stage 1 is characterised by the gathering of information and increased differentiation within the child's normal classroom work. Assessing pupils' existing knowledge, understanding and basic skills is a fundamental requirement. Pupils make sense of what is new to them in terms of what they already know, understand and can do. Depending on the learning difficulties experienced, in addition to the basic skills of written, spoken and perhaps graphic communication, areas for assessment might include: progress in the taught curriculum; working with others; organising work: preparing, planning and carrying out tasks to time; information handling: finding, analysing, presenting information; and forming and testing suppositions and attitudes to learning. The purpose of assessment is to inform teachers and learners how to plan for effective teaching and learning.

The class teacher may decide in consultation with the special educational needs coordinator that the child could benefit from a period of special attention and, in particular, differentiated teaching within his or her normal classroom work. To be successful, planned teaching approaches must be pupil-centred in that they are based on the understanding and matching of learning and teaching needs from the information gained during the assessment process. Assessment to inform future teaching and learning establishes what a child already knows and can do. There must then be negotiation over the pace of learning, flexible learning tasks and activities which adjust to the pupil's needs. A regular review between individual pupils and teachers to establish the progress made and to inform the next steps in learning is an essential component.

Special educational needs coordinators are responsible for advising and supporting those who will teach the child. In particular, these coordinators are increasingly expected to have a whole-school role in supporting and advising colleagues over differentiation. This of necessity involves work alongside colleagues and includes some monitoring of planning, class organisation and teaching methods and styles for meeting the needs of all pupils in the classroom. Clark *et al.* (1995) found that special needs coordinators supporting pupils in colleagues' classrooms provided them with the opportunity to demonstrate particular techniques and strategies in a helpful and professional way. However, class teachers of younger pupils are often confident in their own knowledge and skills as teachers but want advice that increases their ability to meet individual needs within ordinary classes (Richmond and Smith 1990). Help with the assessment of pupils' difficulties, advice on individual teaching programmes and the provision of appropriate teaching materials is particularly helpful. Practical and school-based inservice training on responding to pupils' special needs in the classroom is valued by class teachers.

All actions under Stage 1 should be recorded. The Code of Practice (DFE 1994b) suggests that records might include: the nature of the concern about the progress of the child and the action to be taken; the learning targets to be achieved; arrangements for monitoring progress; and a date on which progress will be formally reviewed. Parents should always be informed of the action that the school proposes to take and the date for the review. The self-monitoring school will have the arrangements in place to ensure that the planning of any special arrangements and the pupil's progress are properly recorded. It is this information that will form the basis of the review of the success or otherwise of the special provision that has been made.

INDIVIDUAL EDUCATIONAL PLANNING

Provision for those pupils with individual needs at Stages 2 and 3 on the register is characterised by the production of an individual educational plan. At Stage 3 the individual educational planning is advised by the contribution of specialists or professionals from outside school. The special educational needs coordinator working with the child's class teacher and any relevant curriculum specialists now ensures that an individual educational plan is drawn up. It has three key aspects: the learning difficulties experienced; the programme of intervention; and the outcomes. The features of an individual education plan appear as figure 6.3 on page 115.

The Code of Practice recommends that as far as possible the plan should build on the curriculum the child is following alongside fellow pupils and should make use of programmes, activities, materials and assessment techniques readily available to the child's teachers. The plan should usually be implemented, at least in part, in the normal classroom setting. The special educational needs coordinator should therefore ensure close liaison between all relevant teachers. The parents should always be informed of:

• the action the school proposes to take
• any help they can give their child at home
• the review date

The purpose of an individual educational plan is to inform teaching and learning and it is unlikely to do this unless copies are given to the staff concerned with putting the plan into action, and to pupils and parents. OFSTED (1996b) found that individual educational plans for Stages 2 and 3 are often too long and too demanding and suggested that they should be short-term working documents.

The process of individual educational planning is very similar to that involved in the recording of achievement (Richmond 1994). It involves a cyclical process in which current learning is assessed, targets for future learning are negotiated and agreed with the learner, criteria for the achievement of the targets are established, a course of learning is pursued and evidence of progress collected. A self-review then takes place supported by teachers, peers, parents and other adults, and achievements are recorded. New learning targets are agreed and so the process continues. Adequate time for review involving the learner is essential for success and should be planned as part of the school policy on assessment, recording and reporting. As Halliwell (1995) states, all assessment of pupils with special needs should be an extension of the school's work with all pupils. Pupils and teachers need to develop appropriate skills to ensure the full benefits of the self-review of progress. If the school operates recording of achievement properly the process of individual educational planning will fit well inside established procedures.

To be useful to both the teacher and the pupil learning targets should conform to some simple rules. It is important that targets should specify: first, what the pupil should be able to do or produce; second, the circumstances in which the pupil should be able to do it; third, the criteria to be used to judge success. There are a number of ways of establishing the sequence of learning targets. Some approaches assume that knowledge or skills are hierarchical, others that skills are clustered (NFER 1995). Most teachers used lists of small steps as an aid to curriculum planning. Norwich (1995) adopts a broad and flexible attitude to what constitutes learning targets: from 'specific objectives in observable learner outcome terms from which specific teaching strategies can be derived' to 'sets of related and more general objectives linked to general teaching procedures or learning encounters based on general teaching principles with expected outcomes of only the most general kind'. Norwich lists the characteristics of good targets as: attainable and practical; related to other learning targets; significant for the individual pupil; and able to be assessed so that learning progress can be judged.

Learning targets must not be so inflexible that there is no chance of adapting them to the needs, interests and experiences of the individual pupil. The self-monitoring school will recognise that the goals of education are broader than learning objectives or learning targets. The Warnock Report (DES 1978: 1.4) specified the goals of education as:

> first to enlarge a child's knowledge, experience and imaginative understanding and thus awareness of moral values and capacity for enjoyment; and secondly to enter the world after formal education is over as an active participant in society and a responsible contributor to it, capable of achieving as much independence as possible.

Learning targets should not be established as an alternative or separate curriculum for individual pupils, but be understood in the context of the whole-curriculum experience of the pupil in the school.

REVIEWING PROGRESS

In the self-monitoring school all pupils, including those with special needs, will be involved in assessing, recording and reporting their progress and in gathering the evidence. Williams and Bowring (1993) identify a number of ways in which pupils can be involved: by being made aware of what they need to learn, what they are expected to provide as evidence, what they know, and what they need to do next. Prompt sheets are helpful to pupils. OFSTED (1995c) recognise that 'records of achievement have done much in primary schools to cultivate pupils' assessments of their own achievements'.

The Code of Practice (DFE 1994b) suggests that a meeting convened by the school special educational needs coordinator to review the progress of pupils with individual educational plans should take place at least twice a year. The review should focus on:

- the progress made by the child
- the effectiveness of the education plan
- updated information and advice
- future action and in the case of pupils at Stage 3 on the school special educational needs register whether the child is likely in future to be referred for statutory assessment

Parents should always be invited to, encouraged to attend and told the outcomes of Stage 3 reviews. Where there is any question of the child being referred to the LEA for statutory assessment, parents should always be consulted in person.

The self-monitoring school will be aware of the relationship between the progress that pupils make and the degree of parental interest in the education of their children (DES 1964) and therefore be convinced of the value of parental involvement. Wolfendale (1995) provides substantial evidence of the value of parental partnership with schools. The Department for Education, concerned that parents of children with special needs get the information they require, has produced two booklets for parents (DFE 1994c and 1994d). The Code of Practice (DFE 1994b: 1.2) recognises that:

the knowledge, views and experience of parents are vital. Effective assessment and provision will be secured where there is the greatest possible degree of partnership between parents and their children and schools.

Strategies for involving the parents of children with special needs will be an extension of the arrangements for all parents and start at an early stage. Information for parents on school arrangements to meet special needs, and copies of individual educational plans to which they have been encouraged to contribute, should be the starting point for greater parental involvement. The self-monitoring school will, for example: act upon parents' concerns; record agreed parental views; involve the parent in helping the child; give copies of reports to parents; and advise parents on keeping records themselves. It will also prepare parents and pupils to contribute to review meetings, keep a record of them and ensure that individual educational plans are complete as a result of reviews.

FORMAL ASSESSMENT OF PUPILS' NEEDS

If by the second Stage 3 review a child's progress is not satisfactory, the headteacher, on the advice of the special educational needs coordinator, should consider advising the LEA that a statutory assessment might be necessary. The written information and evidence required by the LEA on referral for a statutory assessment is likely to be that shown in figure 6.4 on page 116.

Pupils are registered at Stage 4 both when they have been referred for a formal assessment and when a formal assessment is taking place. This period could be twenty-six weeks or more if the LEA takes time to decide that a statutory assessment may be necessary. During this time the educational needs of pupils must not be ignored. The self-monitoring school would not allow referral for a statutory assessment to excuse the school from continuing to respond to the learning needs of any pupil, and this would include the continuation of individual educational planning.

Pupils with statements of their special needs are placed on the register at Stage 5. Additional resources may be attached to statements. Any additional teaching or non-teaching staff have to be inducted into the school policies and procedures, their role managed and monitored. OFSTED (1996a: 5) found that the 'most influential factor on the effectiveness of in-class support is the quality of joint planning of the work between class teacher and the support teacher or special support assistant (SSA)'. The self-monitoring school will have a clear policy on the role of support staff including special support assistants, their contribution to pupil learning, the planning required of them and the records of their work which they are expected to keep (Fox 1994). However, not all statements have additional resources attached to them. The Code of Practice (DFE 1994b: 4.11) contains some examples of provision for pupils on statements which a school 'could reasonably be expected to make out of its own resources':

- occasional advice from an external expert
- occasional support with personal care from a non-teaching assistant
- access to a piece of equipment such as a portable word processor, electronic keyboard or a tape recorder
- minor building alterations such as widening a doorway or improving the acoustic environment

LEAs have the power to review a statement at any time during the year but must review within twelve months of making a statement or of a previous review. It is the LEA's responsibility to initiate the annual statutory review and they are required to give headteachers two months' notice of the date by which the report of the review must be returned to the LEA. The self-monitoring school will have established procedures for reviews. The headteacher must convene the review meeting and invite a representative of the LEA, the child's parents, and a teacher with responsibility for the education of the child. Written advice must be sought from all concerned and a copy of all the advice received must be circulated two weeks prior to the review meeting inviting additional comments. The purpose of the review is to assess the child's progress against the objectives in the statement and towards any agreed learning targets, to review the provision made, to consider the continuing appropriateness of the statement and to set new targets for the coming year.

Parents and pupils should be encouraged to be actively involved in the statutory review process, including attendance at the review meeting. Both parents and pupils should be helped in preparing their contributions. A copy of the headteacher's review report which includes an account of the review meeting must be sent to the LEA by the specified date. For the self-monitoring school the annual statutory review and the review report are very important events in informing the future educational provision and learning targets for the pupil. The self-monitoring school will ensure that pupils with statements will have individual educational plans informed by both the statement and the statutory annual reviews. In the self-monitoring school the preparation of the review report will be part of the established procedures for individual educational planning, reviews of plans and the records of progress kept.

THE EFFECTIVENESS OF SCHOOL POLICIES AND PROCEDURES

Governing bodies of all maintained schools are required under Part III of the Education Act 1993 to publish information about the schools' policy on special educational needs. The Education (Special Educational Needs Information 1994) Regulations prescribe the information to be made available: about the school's special educational provision; about the school's policies for the identification, assessment and provision for all pupils with special educational needs; and about the school's staffing policies and partnership with bodies beyond the school. Governing bodies also have a statutory duty to include within the annual governors' report to parents and for discussion at the annual parents' meeting (DES 1992) a report on: the success of the school's special needs policy; any significant changes in the policy; the outcome of any consultations with the LEA or the Funding Authority for Schools (FAS); and how resources have been allocated to pupils with special educational needs.

EVALUATING THE SUCCESS OF THE POLICY

Guidance (DFE 1994a) suggests that the writing of the annual report offers governing bodies a regular opportunity to reflect on the success of the school's policy and to assess the effectiveness of that policy against its broad principles and objectives. Schools may wish to use the annual report to alert parents to the availability of the full special needs policy which should include a section on how the governing body evaluate the success of the education which is provided at the school to these pupils (DFE 1994a). OFSTED (1996a) found that fewer than half the schools visited had appropriate arrangements in place to monitor policy and practice for pupils with special needs and one-quarter of the schools had no arrangements. The special needs policy in the self-monitoring school will clearly state the procedures for evaluating the working of the policy and what evidence is to be collected. The methods might include:

- details of what is to be observed
- which records should be scrutinised and what for
- what is to be counted
- what minutes of meetings are to be kept and in what form
- how the allocation and use of resources is to be recorded

It is for the self-monitoring school to devise a clear strategy. Behind the contents of the governors' report will be information from the monitoring of the working of the special needs policy, gathered systematically over the year by the school's special needs coordinator. The self-monitoring school will be observing and recording information about the operation of the policy to judge if the school is carrying out the agreed procedures and to evaluate the success of those procedures for the education of individuals and groups of pupils with special educational needs.

Evidence to evaluate the success or otherwise of the special needs policy should be gathered about: the arrangements for the identification of pupils; the assessment procedures; the provision for individuals and groups of children; and the monitoring and recording of their progress. The contribution of outside support services and agencies should be monitored and recorded. Any staff development planned to increase whole-school awareness and to improve the skill of staff in matching work to learning needs should be documented and carefully evaluated for the effect on professional practice in the school. Some questions to enable the evaluation of the success of the special educational needs policy by the self-monitoring school appear in figures 6.5A and 6.5B on pages 117–18.

The governors are required to report any significant changes to the school policy, but even relatively insignificant changes resulting from monitoring can make an important difference to the effectiveness of the policy and practice: for example, changes to record sheets, availability of teaching materials, access to information technology, the pattern of meetings, the monitoring of individual educational plans and specialist accommodation for special educational needs. Significant changes could be a change of special needs coordinator, changes to methods of identifying pupils, the responsibilities of class teachers or subject coordinators, arrangements for staff development, admission of pupils with learning difficulties, the conduct and recording of the decisions of meetings, pupil groupings for the curriculum as they affect pupils with special educational needs, arrangements for referring pupils as cause for concern, funding arrangements and changes to the frequency of visits by the school psychologist or support teacher.

The self-monitoring school will use the evidence gathered to evaluate provision and to form a view about how the policy and provision might become more effective. Monitoring is a formative process and the purpose is to enable informed changes to be made to professional beliefs, practices and procedures. Torrington *et al.* (1988) identify Key Stages in effecting change. The first stage involves collecting facts about whether a change is needed. The next stage involves consultation with those affected and those interested. The implementation of the planned change follows. A final follow-up stage involves monitoring progress and arrangements for some formal feedback on the effectiveness of the changes. Any proposed changes should be planned, managed and again evaluated in a systematic manner. The questions in figure 6.6 on page 119 are helpful.

ALLOCATION AND USE OF RESOURCES BY THE SCHOOL

Local management of schools has devolved funding from LEAs to schools following the implementation of the Education Reform Act (DES 1988a). Dee (1992) identifies the effect of this on trends in special education needs provision. Mainstream schools are called upon and expected to take responsibility for providing for pupils' special needs. With the delegation of special needs resources to schools have come reductions in support services and specialist teaching provided by the LEAs. With the budget comes responsibility and accountability. OFSTED (1996a) identified a developing awareness amongst schools of the delegated funding available for special educational needs, and this knowledge improved the monitoring of provision within schools. Clark *et al.* (1995) found that innovatory practice in primary schools was associated with the identification of resources dedicated to special needs by headteachers and governing bodies. Schools were able to identify staffing and resource rooms dedicated to special needs. The school which is clearly concerned about responding to the learning needs, interests and capacities of all the pupils who attend the school, valuing all pupils equally, will want to allocate resources fairly to meet the diversity of needs.

In law, a special need is defined as a learning difficulty which requires additional resources over and above those normally available (DFE 1994a). Pupils with special needs are entitled to their share of the devolved budget along with all the other pupils registered at the school. In addition there may be funds devolved to the school on the basis of the incidence of under-achievement, learning difficulty or special needs in the school population. It is entirely at the discretion of governing bodies as to how this money is allocated; but the school special needs policy must state how resources are allocated to pupils with special educational needs and will at least involve plans for the deployment of teaching and non-teaching staff and any specialist equipment or materials. Often the resources previously spent centrally on support services for pupils with reading and learning difficulties are also in school budgets somewhere. The school governing body has the responsibility for providing for special needs and allocating appropriate resources to do this.

The governors of the self-monitoring school will be recording all decisions relating to resources for meeting special needs in the school. The National Association of Head Teachers has provided some guidance (NAHT 1995) on establishing and monitoring existing spending on special needs. Bentley (1995) discusses resource allocation and the definition of special needs but also includes some practical suggestions for agreeing a budget and allocating additional resources. The justification for the actual allocation of additional resources to special needs in the school must be based on the school monitoring systems of the progress and needs of pupils with learning difficulties and, as discussed previously, the efficiency with which the resources available are used. Although not current guidance, the 1994 amendment to the *Handbook for the Inspection of Schools*, Technical Paper 8 (OFSTED 1994) included some questions for independent inspectors to consider when evaluating the allocation of resources for pupils with special needs. The questions, reproduced in figure 6.7 on page 120, are still pertinent.

THE ANNUAL PARENTS' MEETING

The public accountability of the school for the provision for pupils with special needs does not end when the governors' annual report goes home to parents. Parents are entitled to attend the annual parents' meeting at which the report will be discussed and parents are likely to ask questions and seek further clarification. Governors are required to report back on any resolutions or topics raised. It might be that questions will be asked on the special needs policy and provision in the school. Typical questions at annual parents' meetings are shown in figure 6.8 on page 121.

The self-monitoring school will be well able to anticipate the concerns about, and interest of parents in the school provision. The headteacher of the self-monitoring school will be well informed to answer parents' questions; but, in consultation with the governors, the headteacher might decide that the presence of the special educational needs coordinator who has day-to-day responsibility for the policy and has most likely prepared and supplied the information about the success of the policy would not only be helpful to the discussion and the development of the school policy but also to the professional development of the coordinator him/herself.

MANAGING PROVISION: ACCOUNTABILITY FOR OUTCOMES

The management of provision for pupils with learning difficulties is a key issue for the self-monitoring school. Good management will identify the practices which most effectively lead to success and progress for pupils with learning difficulties. Cooperative ways of working across the school will be encouraged and valued. Ultimately the policy is designed to improve the quality of teaching and learning for all pupils in school by focusing on the learning needs of those experiencing learning difficulties. The governing body has responsibility for carrying out the statutory duties outlined in the Code of Practice (DFE 1994b) and, in cooperation with the headteacher, determines the general policy and approach, establishes appropriate staffing and funding arrangements, and has general oversight of the policy and provision.

The headteacher has responsibility for the day-to-day management, should keep the governing body fully informed and work closely with the school special needs coordinator. It is the lead given by headteachers which is identified by HMCI (OFSTED 1995a) as central to improving teaching in schools. The support and interest of the headteacher is essential if the special needs coordinator is in turn to support teachers across the school in differentiating teaching and learning for pupils.

The special educational needs coordinator has responsibility for the day-to-day operation of the policy and is required to work closely with all the teachers in the school. OFSTED (1996b: 32) found from school inspections that 'where the special needs coordinator is a member of the senior management team of the school and has time to work with subject and support teachers, the learning needs of pupils with learning difficulties are usually well met'. Bentley *et al.* (1994) identify the responsibilities of the coordinator shown in figure 6.9 on page 121.

Moss (1995) breaks down the roles into a 'co-ordinating job', an 'administrative job' and a 'teaching job'. Others (for example, Dyson and Gains 1995) have identified the role of the special needs coordinator as: advocate and reformer responsible for building consensus and confidence; protecting the rights of pupils; developing access to the power structures of the school; and questioning existing practices.

OFSTED (1996a) found that lack of time considerably affected the effectiveness of special needs coordination across primary schools. Special needs coordinators should have time to observe pupils in the classroom. However, for many coordinators there is a conflict between coordinating and teaching. Headteachers and special educational needs coordinators must consider carefully the balance of time given to these activities and establish some priorities and supporting arrangements. If the demands on one person are too great, the self-monitoring school will recognise this and clearly establish some priorities and manageable alternative arrangements.

Procedures are important, but only as a means to an end. The clear focus in the self-monitoring school will be the teaching and learning of pupils with special educational needs and more specifically the progress they make. OFSTED (1996a) identified a key feature of monitoring procedures as regular meetings between the special educational needs coordinator, the class teacher and any support staff to discuss the progress of pupils. A significant feature of the *Framework for the Inspection of Schools* is the emphasis on the observation of lessons. Judgments are firstly concerned with the attainment of and progress that pupils make. The guidance on the inspection of special schools (OFSTED 1995a) gives considerable emphasis to the progress that pupils make. Evidence of that progress is to be found in, for example, the records of pupils' learning, teachers' planning, individual educational plans, statements of special educational needs and the results of reviews. These will be monitored and the school will know and be able to demonstrate that progress.

Figure 6.1 Monitoring the effectiveness of teaching (adapted from NCC 1989: 6)

- Do schemes of work set out the aims and objectives for the curricular area in question?
- Can the tasks and activities be chosen and presented to enable children with a wide range of attainments to experience success?
- Can activities be matched to pupils' differing paces and styles of learning, interests, capabilities and previous experience?
- Can the activities be broken down into a series of small and achievable steps for pupils who have marked learning difficulties?
- Will the activities stretch pupils of whom too little may have been expected in the past?
- Can a range of communication methods be employed with pupils with communication difficulties?
- Will the purpose of activities and the means of achieving them be understood and welcomed by pupils with learning difficulties?
- Are cross-curricular themes, including personal and social education, running through policies?
- Do schemes refer to material resources and to their financial implications?
- How will teaching and special support assistance be deployed?
- Are there clear procedures for assessing, recording, reviewing and evaluating pupils' progress?

Figure 6.2 Good and poor teaching in special schools (adapted from OFSTED 1996a)

Good

- careful lesson planning that takes account of the needs of individual pupils
- skilful questioning
- balance of individual and group work
- pupils challenged by the activities
- pupils working cooperatively and assuming appropriate levels of personal responsibility for their own learning

Poor

- failure to ensure effective deployment of support staff
- little consideration given to matching tasks and activities to pupils' abilities
- insufficient opportunity for pupils to take a degree of personal responsibility for their own learning
- pupils required to listen for unduly long periods and offered too few opportunities to demonstrate their knowledge and understanding
- disruption usually in those lessons when the level of work set is poorly matched to pupils' abilities and little account taken of learning needs

Figure 6.3 The individual education plan (adapted from DFE 1994b: 4: 11(i))

An individual education plan should set out:

The learning difficulties

- start date and review date
- nature of the child's learning difficulties
- priorities for action

The intervention

- targets to be achieved in a given time
- action plan:

    the special educational provision

    staff involved including frequency of support

    specific programmes, activities, materials, equipment
- help from parents at home
- any pastoral care or medical requirements

The outcomes

- monitoring and assessment arrangements
- review arrangements and date
- next action

Figure 6.4 SEN information likely to be required by LEA (adapted from DFE 1994b: 3: 8)

Information

- educational and other assessments
- views of the parent and the child
- the child's health
- any social services or welfare involvement

Evidence

- the school's intervention under the school-based stages – 1, 2 and 3
- individual education plans for the child
- regular reviews and their outcomes
- involvement of other professionals

Figure 6.5 Evaluating the success of the SEN policy

Identification and assessment

- What are the identification procedures used by the school and are they appropriate?
- How many children are identified by the school at each stage on the register?
- Are the criteria for the identification of pupils appropriate?
- Are the criteria applied consistently?
- Do all staff know who the children with special educational needs are and the nature of their learning difficulties?
- Are the arrangements for assessing pupils consistent with the school assessment, recording and reporting policy?
- Are the results of assessment used to inform curriculum planning for pupils with special needs?

Provision

- What is the balance between support in withdrawal teaching groups and support in the class?
- What is the evidence that the participation of pupils with special educational needs in the educational and social life of the school is increasing?
- What is the evidence that pupils have access to the National Curriculum?
- Are agreed procedures being followed by all concerned?
- In what respects are the arrangements for coordination effective?
- Are individual educational plans effective working documents for the school?
- What do the parents think about the arrangements for their involvement and role?
- What resources have been made available and how have these been used?

© 1997 Robin Richmond

Figure 6.5 Evaluating the success of the SEN policy (cont.)

Monitoring and recording

- How many parental concerns have been recorded?
- What is the evidence for the progress made by individual pupils?
- Have all necessary reviews, including statutory reviews, been carried out as planned?
- In what respects have arrangements for the conduct of reviews been effective/ineffective for planning learning for pupils?
- What more could be done to encourage and support pupils and parents to contribute more effectively to reviews?
- How many meetings have been held, are these justified and do the minutes of meetings record the decisions made?
- What has been the effect on policy and practice of any professional development that has taken place ?

Use of external support services and agencies

- Is there a record of outside agencies used by the school, for example, psychology services, advisory teachers, counsellors?
- On what issues has the school been consulted by the LEA, the FAS or other schools, and for what purposes?
- What links has the school had with pupils and teachers in other schools in the area?

Figure 6.6 Planning, managing and evaluating change

- What is to be done?
- How is it to be done?
- When is it to be done?
- What are the criteria for success?
- Who is the person responsible?
- What is the budget allocation?
- What factors are involved?
- What arrangements are there for monitoring progress?
- What arrangements are there for checking the success of implementation?

Figure 6.7 Allocation of resources for SEN

Efficiency

- Is the LEA's allocation of funds for SEN spent on pupils with SEN?
- How is the weighting for SEN within the LMS formula deployed across the school?
- Are there arrangements in place for monitoring and evaluating this?

Teaching and non-teaching staff

- Are staffing levels sufficient for pupils with SEN?
- Does the SEN coordinator have appropriate status, qualifications and experience?

Resources for learning

- Are equipment and differentiated materials available in classes to support pupils with SEN?
- Do the resources provided for pupils with SEN enable them to gain full access to the whole curriculum?

Figure 6.8 Some questions asked by parents

- Why does it take so long to get a statement of special educational needs?
- I know there are children in school who cannot read. What is the school doing about this?
- Do the teachers have special training to help children with difficulties?
- You do all this for children with special educational needs but what about able children?
- My child is dyslexic and I have given you all the information. Why does he not get any special help?
- I would like to know why you have all these stages?
- Has the school got any computers to help these pupils?
- How many children have special educational needs in this school?

Figure 6.9 Responsibilities of the SEN coordinator (from DFE 1994b: 2: 14)

- the day-to-day operation of the policy
- liaising with and advising the other teachers
- coordinating the provision
- maintaining the special needs register and overseeing records
- liaising with parents of children with special educational needs
- contributing to the inservice training of staff
- liaising with external agencies including educational psychologists, medical and social services and voluntary bodies

Chapter 7

The role of the LEA

David Oakley

David Oakley has been a general inspector in Dudley LEA for eight years. He has subject responsibility for science and environmental education 4–19 and is pastoral adviser to a group of primary schools in central Dudley. Since September 1995 he has been staff inspector with responsibility for monitoring.

Schools do not improve through autonomous self-help or through government edict. They need a combination of both. The challenge of external evaluation cannot be ignored. Schools can benefit from the external perspective and from being part of networks. The critical friend/honest broker role of the LEA has been for the majority of schools an influential factor in the way that they have functioned. The quality of schooling is plainly central to the public education service. Labour and Conservative parties both emphasise the role of the LEA in setting and raising standards. 'Planning and quality assurance' were listed in consultation document 6/94 (Local Government Commission for England 1994) as part of the LEA function. HMCI Woodhead has endorsed that view.

The precise responsibilities of the LEA are, however, a 'grey area'. LEAs interpret statutory provision differently. Clarification of alternative interpretations can only be by amendment of current legislation, new legislation or through judgments in the courts. The proposal to inspect LEAs is likely to generate a debate on what the framework for inspecting them should be. Any framework must include criteria on the LEA's monitoring and quality assurance role against which to evaluate how efficiently and effectively these functions are carried out, and the systems in place for identifying and addressing poor performance and promoting good practice. The Schools Act (DES 1992) set limitations on the general power of the LEA to inspect its schools at large. There is a statutory duty for LEAs to monitor the delivery of the National Curriculum and the implementation of Local Management of Schools by governors. Under the Schools Act (1992) and the Education Act (DES 1993a) LEAs are required to deploy support in the case of schools deemed by OFSTED to require special measures (DFE 1993b). The control required by legislation from 1984 onwards of specific grants, the most significant example being GEST, involves an implied or stated duty to monitor. Some LEAs have collected school development plans as part of this process and in the 1995–6 and 1996–7 cycles schools were required to submit details of their plans for spending the GEST category of 'school effectiveness'. Exactly how LEAs responded to these requirements is not clear. In those LEAs with the facility to provide inservice training the information gained has been useful as a contribution to a needs analysis to shape INSET programmes. Some LEAs have their own development plans and information from schools about their priorities has helped to influence LEA priorities. Information in school development plans has a potential use as part of the LEA's monitoring role. Yet feedback about individual plans has not been widespread and few LEAs have explained how they intended to use the plans, if at all. In the academic year 1996–7 a proportion of the GEST school efficiency category is for retention by the LEA to support schools' post-OFSTED action planning. The main strategy so far evident seems to be to employ further advisory support staff to work with schools.

The role of the LEA as arbiter of GEST funding is likely to disappear or diminish as the Teacher Training Agency takes a lead in the provision of inservice as well as initial teacher training. LEAs may well have to bid against other providers for training provision in a similar market economy to the OFSTED model for inspection of schools. The LEA has had a duty to verify teachers' and national curriculum tasks and test assessments at Key Stage 1. The religious education duties of the LEA extend to grant-maintained schools. There are statutory duties associated with regard to special educational needs provision which have remained despite the erosion of many of the LEA's functions. As early as 1991 the annual report of Her Majesty's Senior Chief Inspector of Schools referred to reductions in the numbers of inspectors/advisers in about a third of LEAs and loss of advisory teachers within the previous two years amounting to 25 per cent.

There are LEAs which take a minimalist view of their responsibilities and monitor for the most part at a distance, only being involved when problems are brought to their attention by the school or as a result of complaints. The 1944 Education Act, still in force, gives scope for another more creative opinion, that 'securing efficient education' requires considerable curricular intelligence and investment in larger rather than smaller numbers of advisory and inspectoral staff. Many LEAs had their own inspection cycles before OFSTED was set up. These 'inspections' usually took the form of reviews which offered advice on ways in which the school could improve, and influenced the deployment of LEA support services. Some LEAs had no experience of anything approaching an inspection model and it was, in part, the perception by government that such LEAs were in a majority that led to the setting up of the OFSTED machine. Schools will be in different positions with regard to LEA provision and thus with different potential to make use of the expertise of LEA staff. Grant-maintained schools are in a similar position to those in LEAs with a minimalist presence and have increasingly turned to consultants to fill the gap left by the lack of LEA provision. The role of the LEA as a 'critical friend' is still part of the established ethos of many LEAs and has survived despite the comparative turmoil of the last few years of corrosive legislation. The 'third survey of LEA advisory and inspection services' (Mann 1995) summarised the trends identified by surveys carried out in 1993 and 1994 as:

- falling numbers of inspectors/advisers/advisory teachers
- increasing LEA involvement in OFSTED inspections
- diminishing advice and support for schools

Other reports from national bodies confirm and often lament these changes. The survey by Mann (1995) received replies from seventy-four LEAs (61 per cent). Only three LEAs (4 per cent) reported substantial increases. Seventy-three per cent indicated an overall reduction in posts, 14 per cent reported losses of more than one half of posts. The total number of inspector/adviser posts declined by 14 per cent, a loss of 230 posts. Advisory teacher posts numbering 434 were lost and 11 per cent of LEAs reported no remaining advisory teacher posts. Almost half of the responding English and Welsh LEAs had fewer than the minimum specified by the Audit Commission (1989) in order to cover the required range of subjects and skills. Contrary to the general decline in curriculum coverage, however, there has been an increase of 2 per cent in inspector/adviser posts for primary education. The trend for a significant proportion of inspector/adviser time to be spent on OFSTED inspections deprives schools of their services but also gives them access to the expertise gained in undertaking these inspections. Sixteen per cent of LEAs in the survey are bidding for all their primary schools. Despite schools' concerns about objectivity - which have proved to be groundless – there are potentially great advantages in this, provided that the LEA then has the capacity to work with the school, post-inspection, on action planning and the necessary follow-up support. The majority of all inspector/advisers are OFSTED team inspectors and 40 per cent are also qualified as OFSTED registered inspectors. Many LEAs now have to raise some of their income by the sale of services to schools, though devolution of funds to schools in such LEAs goes some way to financing service agreements or other buy-back arrangements. Most LEAs feel a great deal of uncertainty about the future. Further reductions in staffing are anticipated in advisory teacher posts, but losses of inspector/adviser posts are generally expected to be marginal.

There is some concen over becoming too dependent on OFSTED as a source of income, and in some LEAs there is a recognition that market-dictated philosophies are becoming outdated. The current debate on school effectiveness and school improvement cannot produce results without using the extensive expertise of LEA advice and inspection services. Two recent studies (Keele University 1995a and 1995b) reveal that most schools still favour their LEAs as providers of professional development services. An individual school should be well aware of what its LEA can offer.

If LEA support is minimal the school may need to obtain the services of a critical friend from among the ranks of consultants, many of whom have recent experience of working for LEAs and current experience of OFSTED inspections. Using consultants can be risky as they tend to function as individuals and lack access to the team expertise that LEA personnel can draw on. Lack of up-to-date experience also inevitably creeps up on consultants. It is vital that schools use trusted networks to vet potential consultants and that they draw up contracts which specify exactly what the process and product of the involvement will be. No matter how effective a school's self-review is, it still needs external, objective validation of that review.

HOW CAN A SCHOOL USE LEA PROVISION TO ESTABLISH GOOD MONITORING PRACTICE?

It is usual for LEAs to have link or pastoral advisers who work with individual schools to provide management and curriculum advice, involvement in staff selection and attendance at governors meetings, either as clerk or the CEO's representative. They have a 'patch' which will vary in size according to the nature of the LEA and the number of inspectors that it can deploy. Availability of inspectors is also likely to vary with the nature of their other commitments but, whatever the situation, the school needs to clarify with the LEA what the entitlement to the school adviser's time is: as an example, the equivalent of five days per year in a well-staffed West Midlands Metropolitan Borough. When the school knows what its allocation is, it can then decide on the best use to be made of the time available. The advisers' experience of the monitoring processes used in other schools that they have worked in or inspected may be worth exploring at the outset. By presenting its planned strategies to the adviser the school may get useful views on the manage-ability of the process, a few short-cuts may be suggested and potential pitfalls avoided. It may be that the relationship with advisers is such that they could play a part in introducing to the staff and governors as part of an INSET session the strategies to be used.

Advisers may be also the best people to train key staff in monitoring techniques, particularly if they can bring experience of OFSTED inspections. The school is likely to be embarking upon self-monitoring strategies as part of the development planning process or action planning in response to an OFSTED inspection.

Development planning will be in the context of a review of the existing development plan or some kind of audit. LEA support and training for development planning has been variable. Some LEAs have concentrated on the documentation, others on the process. Support and training for senior staff and governors have varied and schools will be at different stages of sophistication. Most schools are now aware of the importance of the development plan. Initially it was viewed with scepticism, another extra burden for schools to carry, but has become for many schools a way of pacing the management of change. It is the starting point for OFSTED inspections, and the comments of OFSTED inspectors have enabled schools to refine their own processes and products. Involvement of the school adviser as part of the development plan review exercise can enable the school to satisfy itself that it has sufficient evidence to make judgments about its success or otherwise in meeting the targets set in the school development plan. The adviser's brief could be to respond to those staff reporting on the progress of current initiatives; or the review session could culminate in a presentation to the adviser on the current plan and proposals for the new plan. The adviser could then respond. If an OFSTED action plan is being prepared the focus is likely to be very specific. The range of suggestions for suitable strategies for tackling key issues can be increased by the adviser's knowledge of the school, other schools, OFSTED inspections, the LEA INSET programme and current developments in education. The identification of monitoring strategies will require clarification of the personnel involved, the kind of evidence to be collected and collated, the inferences to be drawn from the evidence and the way any feedback or reporting is to be handled. As well as offering guidance on these elements the services of the adviser can be incorporated into the training aspects identified as part of the planning process. The monitoring skills acquired by advisers as part of their OFSTED experience have added a rigour to their work which was previously the exclusive preserve of HMI. The wealth of experience gained has given LEA advisers a wider perspective of schools, in many cases experience of schools in other authorities. Many, possibly the majority, of LEA advisers and inspectors did not relish the initial, relatively one-sided, nature of OFSTED inspections. The revision of the OFSTED framework has both endorsed the inspector/adviser role, allowing more supportive feedback, and also encourages a greater element of dialogue and discussion with teachers. Labour Party policy is for more support to follow inspection and for LEAs to play a major role in a process which would include school self-evaluation.

OFSTED

The resonance between OFSTED criteria and processes and school self-monitoring has been explored in chapter 1. Involvement of the LEA adviser can ensure that appropriate training takes place in the application of the criteria and that the school particularises them to meet its own requirements. Some consideration needs to be given to how the school's review cycle relates to the OFSTED cycle. Primary schools will have, until the end of the academic year 1997–8, been in the first four-yearly cycle of OFSTED and will have had several months' notice of inspection. The second cycle for secondary schools may result in some schools being inspected more frequently than others. If this system is adopted for primary schools, they should still be able to predict when they are to be inspected, as the criteria for inspection will be published. The self-monitoring school will be well prepared for OFSTED whenever it comes, but it may wish to plan its external validation/evaluation to enable any corrective action to be taken before inspection. Many LEAs are finding that pre-OFSTED preparation is a particularly focused opportunity to work with schools.

On offer are usually:

- INSET on the OFSTED framework
- guidance on how to prepare for OFSTED inspection
- whole-school and subject documentation checks, interviews with post-holders to familiarise them with potential discussion issues
- classroom observation, fed back individually, verbally or in writing or given generically
- training sessions for governors

One LEA has reorganised its own monitoring cycle, overtaken by the OFSTED cycle, as part of pre-OFSTED preparation work with schools. This arrangement debars the advisers involved from then being part of the inspection team. The information obtained advises the LEA on current practice in its schools and helps to shape INSET programmes, contributes to Education Committee reports and the LEA development plan. How the school handles the findings of pre-OFSTED/LEA monitoring activity depends upon how effective their own monitoring and evaluation procedures have been. Good advance planning will enable it to build the findings of the external 'health-check' into the development planning cycle. There is no reason why the action plan required as a statutory response to OFSTED inspection should not begin well before the inspection itself and incorporate any pre-OFSTED preparations and remedial action into it. This will improve the flow of the schools' own programmes of monitoring and also indicate their own willingness to incorporate external validation of the process. Indeed, OFSTED may not always place the same weightings as the school on particular priorities. There is some evidence that schools are 'playing the game' so well during the week of the inspection that the inspection findings under-estimate some areas needing improvement. The OFSTED experience should be seen as potentially the most valuable (and free) consultancy that a school can have; and going up-front with the findings of its own monitoring plans will ultimately be of benefit to the school. Ideally, inspection should be seen as part of an ongoing programme for improvement. Unfortunately the massive anxiety and stress associated with OFSTED subverts attempts to persuade staff of any advantages at all.

Support from the school advisers in the period leading up to and during the course of the inspection week has proved to help morale. They often have the necessary counselling skills and come cheaper than professional counsellors who can cost £250 for a consultation plus £1,000 per day for two people – expenses not included! Adviser attendance at feedback meetings with governors is often important to ensure that judgments are sufficiently well supported by evidence and sufficiently clear to allow action planning to be specifically targeted. Adviser support for action planning can help to focus strategies and can act as a useful link with the governors, whose ultimate responsibility the plan technically is. Action planning has become more sophisticated and schools are now more aware of the importance of monitoring the progress and success of initiatives to bring about improvement.

Some of the early inspections left schools somewhat bewildered about how to plan for improvement. As there is no requirement on the part of OFSTED to respond to those plans, except for schools requiring special measures, there has been relatively little check on how effective action planning is in improving school efficiency. Eighty-five schools inspected in 1993–4 were visited by HMI as part of a survey into action planning. Only twelve were primary schools and these were all inspected by HMI. Action plans were produced voluntarily and not as part of statutory requirements. Arrangements for monitoring and evaluating the progress and impact of the measures taken are quoted as a feature of the best plans; but few schools had developed criteria or indicators against which to monitor and evaluate the effectiveness of the proposed action in terms of raised standards. The recommendations stress the importance of the latter and encourage OFSTED, the (then) DFE and LEAs to give further consideration to 'ensuring that inspection and action planning become more integrated into the ongoing process of school self-review and devel-opment' (OFSTED 1995c). The mid-term OFSTED review is emerging as a useful external check on progress either of the action plan or of what-ever has happened since OFSTED arrived on the scene – whether planned or not! A small team from the LEA, possibly including the school adviser, in a couple of days of focusing on the school's specified targets, can give objective feedback verbally or in writing, which will augment the school's findings, confirming and validating them or giving a direction for future strategies.

THE ROLE OF THE GOVERNORS

The idea of the school as a 'stakeholder society' seeks to express the commitment of all those involved with a school – teachers, governors, parents and, the group least often consulted, the pupils – in quality performance and ways of improvement. There are schools where such an ethos exists, and their unity of purpose is beguiling. But more often than not the partnership is an uneasy one. Stakeholding also implies a degree of empowerment and teachers often feel that quality assurance is something done to them rather than by them. The emphasis by both OFSTED and the school effectiveness movement on the use of particular performance indicators chosen as national yardsticks has tended to subvert the intuitive and informal quality assurance that teachers are more comfortable with. Government policy and media hype focus on accountability rather than partnership.

The empowerment of governing bodies has been a key feature of government policy as a constituent part of LMS legislation and GMS. The role of governing bodies and individual governors is still evolving, and there is a considerable range of practice evident. At one extreme is the 'rubber-stamp' model where the governors simply endorse the proposals of the headteacher and genuinely see this as their role. They seldom, if ever, visit the school during working hours and are content to attend one meeting a term and the annual meeting for parents. The running of the school is left to the 'professionals'. At the other extreme is the governing body which has several committees with clear terms of reference and delegated responsibilities, specified membership, clerking arrangements and quorum, and powers of co-option, and which meet regularly and report back succinctly to meetings of the governing body. Committees can extend open invitations to all governors and publish agenda in advance to enable other governors to contribute to particular items of business. Such governors see themselves as partners with the professionals, fulfilling a complementary role and able to make a positive contribution to the way in which the school works. These governors act as the link with the parents, consulting them in person and through questionnaires. Establishment of this kind of climate is an essential precursor to the acceptance of the role of the governors as monitors. The main aim of the governing body is to maintain and improve the standards of achievement in its school through:

- *Steering*: agreeing policies, setting budgets, agreeing development plans, responding to inspection

- *Monitoring*: plans, budgets, standards of education and achievement
- *Executive role*: admissions, appeals, staff recruitment and selection, discipline
- *Accountability to parents*: annual report, annual meeting, publication of minutes, consultation
- *Support for headteacher*: advice and skills

Fundamental to the process is the way in which the school development plan is prepared and reviewed. Indeed, as all schools should now have a development plan of some description, the review stage is probably the best point of entry for the governing body wishing to increase its involvement in the working of the school. An effective development plan will have clear targets which are prioritised, costed, have indicators of success and named individuals responsible for the implementation and monitoring of the targets. Some longer-term targets should also be included, based on financial forecasts, trends in pupil numbers, staff salaries and the cost of maintenance. This makes the review process and the identification of new targets a manageable task. Strategies for reviewing the school development plan do not automatically involve governors. The headteacher and senior staff are usually the forum for the review, sometimes off the school premises so that they can concentrate on the task in hand. Local teachers' centres can be conducive environments; the headteacher's front room can be cosier, though sticking up the sheets of flipchart or sugar paper on the wall is unlikely to be acceptable. Where review takes place during the school day, governors may find attendance difficult. Planning such events well in advance as part of the school calendar may enable key governors, such as chairs of committees, to be present. If governors are not able to be present, then using staff governors may be the best way of involving the governing body. It may be conceived as part of the role of the staff governor, which can be a tricky one to define.

If the review takes place outside school hours, governor involvement should be easier and one of them may even offer to host it. After the review, the framing of the next school development plan should be led by senior staff, but involve the whole staff and governors. INSET days often provide a suitable opportunity and governors may be invited, as they often are to relevant staff training sessions. The effectiveness of governor participation is enhanced if, in this, as in all contexts of their work with schools, they are attached to a particular year group, phase or subject. If governor participation is not possible, the way in which the plan is presented to them should be carefully considered, if partnership is to have any real meaning. Choice of words is important. To call it a draft school development plan implies that it is not a *fait accompli*, that governors can still exert an influence and that amendment is still possible. The committee structure can be an extremely productive way of involving governors in aspects of the plan in which they will later be able to undertake a monitoring role. Curricular targets can be presented for discussion to the curriculum committee, premises improvements to the buildings committee, any staffing implications to the personnel committee. The finance committee will need to be involved in the costing of the plan. At these meetings key responsibilities for leading the implementation of developments can be decided and also responsibilities for monitoring of progress on development targets. Involvement of governors in monitoring activities is potentially an extremely sensitive issue. The strategies decribed above, including the committee structure, may be alien to a large number of primary schools, but in many ways there is greater potential to establish productive partnerships in primaries than secondaries. The pupils are usually more approachable, the curriculum more accessible, the ambience more welcoming and the scale of the organisation less daunting. Staff are getting used to a greater degree of accountability, though some are not yet welcoming it with open arms. Governors must be seen as allies and not busybodies, lay people with a commitment to support the school, not another tier of criticism. Establishment of a high level of mutual trust between staff, teaching and non-teaching, and governors should be the overriding aim of initiatives promoting the role of governors as monitors. In order to act as monitors, governors will need information. Governor training is well established in LEAs, indeed it is part of their statutory responsibilities. Governing bodies manage the process themselves, agreeing which governors attend particular courses and conferences in order that the governing body as well as individual governors can be kept informed. Feedback from trained governors is a vital part of this process, as is a systematic approach to training. Linking training to the school development plan is an approach which indicates the will of a governing body to take its responsibilities seriously. There is no reason why governor training should not be indicated and costed in the school development plan along with the staff training plan. An aspect of governor training often overlooked is the provision to new governors of information about the school. Induction packs could include the school prospectus, school calendar, plan of the school, staff list, list of governors and their roles, terms of reference of committees, school policies, the LEA governor training programme, a copy of the most recent annual report to parents and the headteacher's most recent termly report as well as the school's articles of government and a copy of *School Governors: a Guide to the Law* (DES 1988b). Local governors' associations and forums are now becoming established and information about these could also be passed on.

Some LEAs have governors' newsletters to keep governors up to date. In many schools, the staff play a key part in keeping governors informed in curriculum matters, presenting brief sessions often as part of or before governors meetings. These sessions help to establish a good relationship between staff and governors, particularly if the setting can be made a fairly informal one with comfortable seating and refreshments laid on. Such sessions also help to particularise to the school any generic training that governors may have had and pave the way for future sessions where the focus is on reports from staff as part of the monitoring process. Reports to governors or committees is probably the commonest monitoring strategy among those governing bodies tackling this issue. Progress on a particular development is presented in writing or in person either by the individual responsible for the implementation of the target, or the person monitoring it. The timing of the report depends on the timescale set for the particular development. Introduction of a mathematics scheme, for example, could involve phased implementation and consequently phased reporting by the maths coordinator. Establishment of a programme of health education at Key Stage 2 might be reported on at the time of the successful completion of the course by the phase coordinator. A schoolwide initiative to foster more independent learning might involve progress reports from the member of staff monitoring, planning and carrying out classroom observations. The role of the committee is not simply to receive a report, but to ask questions and to discuss the findings of the report. This process will be aided by the setting of clear objectives at the planning stage and the involvement of the governors in the planning process. Once a committee has received a report, it is then in a position to present the report, any results of ensuing discussion and any decisions taken, to the full governing body. Involvement in aspects of the curriculum is a relatively new and tentative area which most governors view with trepidation and some bewilderment. Demystification should be the objective of any training and briefing. It is a valuable exercise for staff to have to translate the arcane aspects of the National Curriculum and its assessment into a form that can be understood by a lay individual.

Initiatives on raising standards of achievement will require a wider range of information. Governing bodies may well see monitoring and influencing pupils' achievement as transcending the development planning process, whether pupil performance figures in plan targets or not. In order to make informed judgments, governors will need to have details of teacher assessment results and Key Stage test results in those subjects where this is statutorily required, both for the school and nationally. The headteacher will need to provide the results of any baseline testing done by the school, results of screening tests and any value-added analyses carried out. Information on the socio-economic circumstances of the intake of the school is also valuable in setting the context for consideration of how well pupils are performing. This can be obtained from local census information which is based on wards. It needs to be interpreted with caution as the pupils attending the school may be drawn from wards other than the one the school is located in. Governors who are also teachers in the school or another school can make a contribution to setting discussions on standards of achievement into context. Involvement of the LEA school adviser as part of this exercise would give governors a valuable perspective.

Governors may consider that they need some first-hand experience of how the school is progressing on its development plan and wish to visit the school as part of their monitoring role. This is more likely to be accommodated by staff if governors are regular and supportive visitors to the school and if they have been partners in the development planning process. Schools that have governors attached to classes, year groups, phases, subjects or other aspects of school life are more likely to be in a position successfully to develop and extend governor involvement. Otherwise such visiting may be seen as threatening and unhelpful. Visits to school need to be carefully planned in advance to reduce disruption and misunderstandings to a minimum. Sensitivity needs to be shown over the choice of individual governors. Deployment of parent governors and local councillors may prove to be difficult and such potential difficulties need to be anticipated in the early stages of the development planning process by the headteacher and chair of governors. The purpose of the visit needs to be agreed with the headteacher and chair of governors, and staff and pupils need to understand why the governors are visiting. Governors need to be well briefed. Any questions likely to be asked could easily be notified to staff in advance. Any samples of work or documentation could also be negotiated in advance.

Staff governors have a particularly constructive role to play in the process. They should be able to liaise and possibly act as hosts or sponsors. The status of any feedback also needs to be clear. Initially, feedback should be given to the headteacher. Reporting on the visit to the governing body or committee needs to be strictly in the context of the monitoring of specific development plan targets.

Classroom visiting as part of the monitoring role of governors is unlikely to be a major strand of their role: many schools have yet to establish a culture of visiting by their own senior staff and curriculum leaders. Where there are good and open relations between governors and the school and the governors are seen as trusted partners by the staff there is no reason why they should not extend their involvement.

Budget monitoring may be seen as a more acceptable role for the governing body. Most governing bodies are now used to receiving, amending and approving the budget, approving the annual accounts and any virement required. Defined responsibilities are delegated to the headteacher for day-to-day financial decisions. Monitoring expenditure is one of the main functions of the finance or finance and general purposes committee. The involvement of the headteacher or other senior member of staff responsible for finance is an essential part of the process and the chair of the finance committee is usually chosen from those on the governing body who have some expertise in this area. Priorities for expenditure should be debated as part of the development planning process. The audit commission and OFSTED have provided schools with guidance on financial management in the reports *Keeping Your Balance* (Audit Commission 1993) and *Adding up the Sums* (Audit Commission 1993–4). The latter enables governors to make comparisons between their school and other schools of a similar size in, for example, the proportion of school budgets allocated to teachers' salary costs. The recent edition identifies a variation of 22 per cent between the highest and lowest spending primary schools and a continuing trend for primary schools to employ more classroom assistants. Information on the average pattern of expenditure in locally managed primary schools enables governors to assess whether their school conforms to the national pattern and to consider the reasons for variations and if necessary to propose modifications. Increasingly, staff in schools are being given greater responsibility for monitoring expenditure for which they are responsible, and part of that responsibility is greater accountability. There is an opportunity here for collaboration between the finance committee and the middle managers in the school on ways of monitoring finance to improve the efficiency of all concerned.

Ultimately the question arises: 'What does a governing body do with the information gained through monitoring?' The answer is that it uses it as part of the planning and decision-making process. If a school does not know where it is and how it is functioning, how can it set targets for improvement? Evidence from school effectiveness studies shows that target setting accompanied by monitoring of performance against those targets and subsequent evaluation enables improvements to be realistically planned for and standards raised.

A final thought on 'stakeholders': what is the role of pupils in the monitoring and evaluation process? Some primary schools have introduced school councils to enable pupils' views to be expressed and taken into account. It is an excellent way of fostering responsibility and independence. Pupils can show an impressive maturity with suitable guidance. Could a school development plan be shared with pupils or their representatives? If so, in what form? Is this an idea for those schools which have effectively dealt with every other aspect of evaluation?

Bibliography

Abbott, R., Birchenough, M. and Steadman, S. (1988) *GRIDS School Handbooks*, (second edition, primary and secondary versions) York: Longman for the SCDC.

Alexander, R., Rose, J. and Woodhead, C. (1992) *Curriculum Organisation and Classroom Practice in Primary Schools. A Discussion Paper*, London: DES.

Aspinwall, K., Simkins, T., Wilkinson, J. F. and McAuley, M. J. (1992) *Managing Evaluation in Education: a Developmental Approach*, London: Routledge.

Aubrey, C. (1995) 'Support for SENCOs: quality teaching', *Special Children: Quality for All*, 86: 10–12.

Audit Commission (1989) *Assessing Quality in Education*, London: HMSO.

Audit Commission/HMI (1992a) *Getting in on the Act. Provision for Pupils with Special Educational Needs: the National Picture*, London: HMSO.

Audit Commission/HMI (1992b) *Getting the Act Together. Provision for Pupils with Special Educational Needs. A Management Handbook for Schools and Local Education Authorities*, London: HMSO.

Audit Commission (1993) *Keeping Your Balance*, London: OFSTED.

Audit Commission (1993–4) *Adding up the Sums: 2 and 3*, London: HMSO.

Barber, M., Stoll, L., Mortimore, P. and Hillman, J. (1995) *Governing Bodies and Effective Schools*, London: DFE.

Barth, R. (1990) *Improving Schools from Within*, San Francisco: Jossey-Bass.

Barton, J., Becher, T., Canning, T., Eraut, E. and Knight, J. (1980) 'Accountability and education', in Bush, T. *et al.* (eds) (1980).

Bentley, A (1995) 'Allocation of the school's resources to meet special educational needs', in Stobbs, P. *et al.* (1995).

Bentley, A., Russell, P. and Stobbs, P. (1994) *An Agenda for Action: a Handbook to Support the Implementation of the Special Educational Needs Arrangements in the Education Act 1993*, London: National Children's Bureau.

Bibby, P. (1995) 'Nasty bumps on the statement threshold', London: *TES*, 12 May.

Bolam, R. (ed.) (1982) *School Focused In-Service Training*, London: Heinemann.

Bush, T., Glatter, R., Goodey, J. and Riches, C. (eds) (1980) *Approaches to School Management*, London: Harper and Row.

Bush, T. (ed.) (1990) *Management in Education*, Milton Keynes: The Open University.

Caldwell, B. J. and Spinks, J. M. (1988) *The Self-managing School*, Lewes: The Falmer Press.

Clark, C., Dyson, A., Millward, A. and Skidmore, D. (1995) *Innovatory Practice in Mainstream Schools for Special Educational Needs*, London: HMSO.

Cohen, M. D., March, J. G. and Olsen, J. P. (1972) 'A garbage can model of organisational change', *Administrative Science Quarterly*, 17(1): 1–25.

Cohen, M. D. and March, J. G., (1973) *Leadership and Ambiguity: the American College President*, New York: McGraw Hill.

Coleman, P. and La Rocque, L. (1990) *Struggling to be 'Good Enough': Administrative Practices and School District Ethos*, London: Falmer Press.

Coopers and Lybrand (1988) *Local Management of Schools*, London: HMSO.

Dean, J. (1992) *Organising Learning in the Primary School Classroom* (second edition), London: Routledge.

Dearing, Ron (1993) *The National Curriculum and Its Assessment*, London: School Curriculum and Assessment Authority.

Dee, C. (1992) 'Formula funding and resourcing for special educational provision' in Evans, J. and Lunt, I., *Developments in Special Education under LMS*, London: ULIE.

DES (1964) *Children and their Primary Schools. A Report of the Central Advisory Council for Education (England)*, London: HMSO.

DES (1978) *Special Educational Needs: Report of the Committee into the Education of Handicapped Children and Young People* (The Warnock Report), London: HMSO.

DES (1985) *Better Schools* (Cmnd 8836), London: HMSO.

DES (1988a) *Education Reform Act*, London: HMSO.

DES (1988b) *School Governors: a Guide to the Law*, London: HMSO.

DES (1990) *Developing School Management: the Way Forward* (a report by the School Management Task Force), London: HMSO.

DES (1992) *Education (Schools) Act Sections 9 and 10*, London: HMSO.

DFE (1993a) *Education Act 1993*, London: HMSO.

DFE (1993b) *Schools Requiring Special Measures* (Circular 17/93), London: HMSO.

DFE (1994a) *The Organisation of Special Educational Provision* (Circular 6/94), London: DFE.

DFE (1994b) *Code of Practice on the Identification and Assessment of Special Educational Needs*, London: DFE.

DFE (1994c) *Special Educational Needs: a Guide for Parents*, London: DFE.

DFE (1994d) *Special Educational Needs Tribunal: How to Appeal*, London: DFE.

Dickinson, C. and Wright, J. (1993) *Differentiation: a Practical Handbook of Classroom Strategies*, Coventry: National Council For Educational Technology.

Dyson, A. and Gains, C. (1995) 'The role of the special needs coordinator: poisoned chalice or crock of gold?', *Support for Learning*, 10(2): 50–6.

Fox, G. (1994) *A Handbook for Special Needs Assistants. Working in Partnership with Teachers*, London: Fulton.

Greenfield, T.B. (1973) 'Organisations as social inventions: rethinking assumptions about change', *Journal of Applied Behavioural Science*, 9(5): 551–74.

Halliwell, M. (1995) 'SEN and a whole school approach to assessment', in Stobbs, P. *et al.* (1995).

Hargreaves, D., Hopkins, D., Leask, M., Connolly, J. and Robinson, P. (1989) *Planning for School Development*, London: DES.

Hargreaves, D. and Hopkins, D. (1991) *The Empowered School*, London: Pan Books.

Hart, S. (1995) 'Differentiation and equal opportunities', in Stobbs, P. *et al.* (1995).

HMSO (1989) *School Teacher Appraisal: a National Framework*, London: HMSO.

Hopkins, D.(1994) 'Process indicators for school improvement', in Tuijman, A. (ed.) *Educational indicators*, Paris: OECD.

Hopkins, D. and Wideem, M.(1984) *Alternative Perspectives On School Improvement*, Lewes: Falmer Press.

Hopkins, D., Ainscow, M., and West, M. (1994) *School Improvement in an Era of Change*, London: Cassell.

Keele University (1995a) *For Better, for Worse: Professional Development Trends in Primary Education*, Keele: Keele University Publications.

Keele University (1995b) *The Glass and the Reality: Managing Professional Development in Secondary Schools*, Keele: Keele University Publications.

Local Government Commission for England (1994) *Summary of Authorities' Current Functions* (Consultation Leaflet 6/94), London: HMSO.

Louis, K.S. and Miles, M.B. (1990) *Improving the Urban High School: What Works and Why*, New York: Teachers College Press.

McMahon, A., Rolam, R., Abbott, R. and Holly, P. (1984) *Guidelines for Review and Internal Development in Schools*, York: Longman/School Council.

Mann, P. (1995) *Third Survey of LEA Advisory and Inspection Services*, Slough: NFER.

March, J.G. (1974) 'Analytical skills and the university training of educational administrators', *Journal of Educational Administration*, 12(1): 17–44.

Mittler, P. and Pumfrey, P. (1989) 'Peeling off the label', London: *TES*, 13 October.

Mortimore, P., Sammons, P., Stoll, L., Lewis, D. and Ecob, R. (1988) *School Matters*, London: Open Books.

Moss, G. (1995) 'A strategy for differentiation', *Special Children: Quality For All*, 86: 10–12.

NAHT (1995) *Guideline 2. Special Educational Provision. The Code of Practice. The School Policy on Special Education*, Haywards Heath: National Association of Headteachers.

NCC (1989) *Curriculum Guidance 2. A Curriculum for All. Special Educational Needs in the National Curriculum*, York: NCC.

NFER (1995) *Small Steps of Progress in the National Curriculum. Final Report: Executive Summary*, Slough: National Foundation for Educational Research.

Nias, J. (1980) 'Leadership styles and job satisfaction in primary schools', in Bush, T. *et al.* (eds) (1980).

Norwich, B. (1995) 'Individual education plans – IEPs', in Stobbs, P. *et al* (1995).

OFSTED (1993a) *Access and Achievement in Urban Education*, London: HMSO.

OFSTED (1993b) *Curriculum Organisation and Classroom Practice in Primary Schools. A Follow-up Report*, London: OFSTED.

OFSTED (1993c) *Handbook of Inspection for Schools*, London: HMSO.

OFSTED (1994) *Improving Schools*, London: OFSTED.

OFSTED (1995a) *Framework for the Inspection of Schools*, London: HMSO.

OFSTED (1995b) *The Handbook of Inspection for Schools*, London: HMSO.

OFSTED (1995c) *Planning Improvement: Schools' Post-inspection Action Plans*, London: HMSO.

OFSTED (1995d) *The Annual Report of HMCI Part 1: Standards and Quality in Education 1993/4*, London: HMSO.

OFSTED (1996a) *Standards and Quality in Education 1994/5. The Annual Report of Her Majesty's Chief Inspector of Schools*, London: HMSO.

OFSTED (1996b) *Subjects and Standards. Issues for School Development Arising from OFSTED Inspection Findings 1994–95 Key Stages 1 and 2. A Report from the Office of Her Majesty's Chief Inspector of Schools*, London: HMSO.

Peters, T. (1987) *Thriving on Chaos: Handbook for Revolution*, London: Pan Books.

Pollard, A. and Tann, S. (1987) *Reflective Teaching in the Primary School*, London: Cassell.

Poster, C. and Poster, D. (1993) *Teacher Appraisal: Training and Implementation* (second edition), London: Routledge.

Reynolds, D. (1982) 'The search for effective schools', *School Organisation*, 2(3): 215–37.

Reynolds, D. and Creemers, B. (1990) 'School effectiveness and school improvement: a mission statement', *School Effectiveness and School Improvement*, 1: 1–3.

Richmond, R. C. (1994) 'The code of practice in schools: learning from recording of achievement', *British Journal of Special Education*, 21(4): 157–60.

Richmond, R. C. and Smith, C. J. (1990) 'Support for special needs: the class teacher's perspective', *Oxford Review of Education*, 16(3): 295–310.

Riley, K. A. and Nuttall, D. L. (1994) *Measuring Quality: Educational Indicators: United Kingdom and International Perspectives*, London: Falmer Press.

Rodger, I. A. and Richardson, J. A. S. (1985) *Self-Evaluation for Primary Schools*, London: Hodder and Stoughton.

Rumbold, A. (1989) in *TES*, 8 December.

Rutter, M., Maughan, B., Mortimore, P. and Ouston, J. (1979) *Fifteen Thousand Hours, Secondary Schools and Their Effects on Children*, London: Open Books.

Sammons, P., Hillman, J. and Mortimore, P. (1995) *Key Characteristics of Effective Schools: a Review of School Effectiveness Research*, London: OFSTED.

Stenhouse, L. (1975) *An Introduction to Curriculum Research and Development*, London: Heinemann.

Stobbs, P., Mackey, T., Norwich, B., Peacey, N. and Stephenson, P. (1995) *Schools' Special Educational Needs Policies Pack*, London: National Children's Bureau.

Stradling, R., Saunders, L. and Weston, P. (1991) *Differentiation in Action. A Whole School Approach to Raising Attainment*, London: HMSO.

Torrington, D., Weightman, J. and Johns, K. (1988) *Management Methods*, London: London Institute of Personnel Management.

Weber, M. (1947) *The Theory of Social and Economic Organisation*, New York: Free Press.

Weston, P. (1992) 'A decade for differentiation' in Peter, M., *Differentiation: Ways Forward*, Stafford: NASEN.

Williams, M. and Bowring, M. (1993) *Records Of Achievement in Primary Schools. A Development and Support Pack for Schools*, Cardiff: Curriculum Council for Wales and the Welsh Joint Education Committee.

Wolfendale, S. (1995) 'Parental involvement', in Stobbs, P. *et al* (1995).

Index